FOOTBALL GROUNDS

from the air *Then* & NOW

Ian Allan
PUBLISHINC

Previous page: City of Manchester Stadium. (697230)
Above: Shrewsbury Town. (697455)
Right: Wembley. (697409)

Front cover: The changing face of Stamford Bridge.

First published 1998
Second edition 2001
Third edition 2004

ISBN 0 7110 3012 X

Published by Ian Allan Publishing

an imprint of Ian Allan Publishing Ltd, Molesey Road, Hersham, Surrey KT12 4RG
Printed by Ian Allan Printing Ltd, Molesey Road, Hersham, Surrey KT12 4RG.

Code: 0409/C2

Contents

Introduction

In the past 30 years the face of football in the British Isles has changed radically. Partly this is the result of legislation, such as the Safety of Sports Grounds Act of 1975, and partly it is a result of changed regulations following two major disasters — Bradford in 1985 and Hillsborough in 1989 — which radically altered the standards to which grounds were expected to meet. Undoubtedly many grounds in the pre-Popplewell and pre-Taylor eras were long past their prime; crumbling terraces, inadequate toilet facilities and poor maintenance were symptomatic of a sport that was, in many ways, in decline. In terms of the current position at most grounds, it is the Taylor Report, issued in 1990, that has had the greatest impact.

As a result of the Taylor Report, stringent new safety regulations were brought in. In particular, the demand that all football grounds be converted to an all-seater format has radically altered the nature of football. Initially, all Premiership and First Division teams were to become all-seater by August 1994 with any teams being promoted to achieve that status within three years of reaching the First Division; it is the latter regulation that saw the end of Bradford City's Kop — probably the largest terracing then still extant in English football — in 1999. In the event, a small number of clubs — primarily those that were hoping to relocate — were granted an extension. Second and Third Division grounds were expected to become all-seater by 1999; in the event, the then Sports Minister (David Mellor), announced in mid-1992 that teams in the lower two divisions could retain standing accommodation, provided that other safety standards were met. It was also decided that all lower division grounds should meet certain criteria in terms of total accommodation and availability of seating; a capacity of 6,000 with 2,000 seated was to become the base figure. Initially a number of aspiring teams from the Conference failed to meet this level, but most of the likely candidates for promotion have now reached it.

The photographs in this book are drawn from a photographic archive stretching back some 85 years. In more than eight decades the face of football has changed dramatically; in many cases the changes wrought have, however, occurred over a relatively recent time with many grounds being largely unchanged from their origins until the post-Taylor era. The huge capacities of the era around World War 2 cannot be replicated; the trend to all-seater stadia and other safety measures has reduced ground capacities although the ever ambitious Manchester United's plans for the continuing redevelopment of Old Trafford will ultimately see the ground's capacity exceed the pre-Taylor record and other new grounds proposed — such as those for Arsenal and Liverpool — will also be considerably larger than the grounds being replaced. The era of uncovered terracing (and seating in certain cases) is gradually coming to an end. Traditional homes with long histories — such as Southampton's The Dell, Stoke's Victoria Ground and Sunderland's Roker Park — are now as much a part of history as other famous venues, replaced by new state-of-the-art grounds, and other famous grounds, such as Anfield, Goodison Park and Highbury are also under threat.

It is to be hoped that the selection of photographs included in this book will provide a graphic reminder of the many famous grounds that have played host to football in England and Wales; many of these grounds are now radically different. It is only through photographs and the memories of the fans that they can be recalled. Although it is only three years since the second edition of this book was published, the extent of changes wrought at the Premiership and Football League grounds over the period is quite frightening. With further new grounds proposed and redevelopment continuing elsewhere, the face of football will continue to evolve.

The unique Aerofilms reference number is indicated together with the date each photograph was taken.

FULHAM: 2004 (697367)

Arsenal

Then: 28 September 1932
Now: 26 May 2001

Whilst there are an increasing number of clubs that have relocated within their own district, few match the change that saw Arsenal move from southeast London to Highbury in 1913. Founded in 1886 as Royal Arsenal and becoming Woolwich Arsenal before joining the Football League in 1893, by March 1910 the club was in dire straits and, in that month, went into voluntary liquidation. The club was rescued by Henry Norris, who controlled Fulham and saw in a merger between the two clubs the opportunity of bringing First Division football to Craven Cottage. In the event, the merger did not proceed but relocation did. After a somewhat hurried period of construction, the new Arsenal Stadium, as Highbury should be referred to, opened on 6 September 1913. It boasted — if that is the right word — a Main (East) Stand designed by Archibald Leitch and open terracing on the three other sides; this had been constructed using spoil from the construction of the Piccadilly Line and by levelling the pitch.

The first of these two pictures shows the ground during its transition from ugly duckling to beautiful swan. These were the years of Herbert Chapman's management when the ground was transformed. In 1931, under the aegis of the architect Claude Waterlow Ferrier, both end terraces were enlarged and, in 1932, the superb West Stand was completed; the new stand was opened officially on 10 December 1932. This is the stage that the earlier photograph records. The North Bank was covered in 1935. After this, the old Main Stand was demolished (in April 1936) and the new stand, similar in style to the West Stand, was designed by William Binnie and opened on 24 October 1936.

Highbury is today still recognisable as the ground that developed in the 1930s; both the East and West stands are still extant, although have been converted to all-seater accommodation. More controversial, however, were the construction of the executive boxes and roof at the Clock End in 1989 — the latter not providing complete protection for the seats installed in November 1993 when Highbury became all-seater — and the demolition of the famous North Bank (in May 1992) and its replacement with the new North Bank Stand which opened on 14 August 1993. The original North Bank roof dated back to 1954 and was a postwar replacement for the 1935 structure destroyed during the war.

As it stands today, Highbury has an all-seater capacity of 38,900. This, the club has decided, is inadequate and Arsenal would have liked to increase it. The problem for the Gunners was that rebuilding was not straightforward. Firstly, parts of the ground are now listed and, secondly, the local residents have objected to any redevelopment and the council was not sympathetic. These problems have led Arsenal to the decision that the club must relocate and, during the 1999/2000 season, it was announced that the club would move to a new 60,000-seat ground at nearby Ashburton Grove. However, the original time-scale proved overly optimistic — it was originally believed that the ground would be completed by the start of the 2003/04 season — as problems over funding the £400 million scheme arose. It is now planned that the new ground will be open for the 2006/07 season and that the existing Highbury will then be redeveloped (with the listed sections being incorporated into any new buildings).

Inset: 1932 (C19089)
Right: 2001 (688308)

Aston Villa

Then: 3 November 1951
Now: 15 June 2004

There were few more impressive sights in British football than the splendour of the Trinity Road facade at Villa Park and it was to the club's credit that this facade was retained until comparatively recently. Drawing inspiration from the grandeur of the nearby Aston Hall, the facade was a glowing tribute to the ambition of the Victorian advocates of professional football — in Villa's case Fred Rinder who, along with Archibald Leitch, did much to shape the ground as seen in the first of these two photographs.

Villa's origins date back to the 1870s and, for a period, the club played at the Lower Meadows, the site of the future Villa Park, before being based until 1896 at Perry Barr. The club's first game back at the Lower Meadows was on 17 April 1897, by which date the Witton Lane Stand, with its three barrel-shaped gables and 1914-built terrace in front, and the end banking were already in place. The scene portrayed in this 1951 photograph shows clearly the lines of the Trinity Road Stand which was built between 1922 and 1924; although it was first used on 26 August 1922 it was not officially opened until 26 January 1924. At either end, the two banks shows the result of extensions undertaken immediately prior to World War 1 along with a further extension to the Holte End completed in February 1940.

As can be seen, the modern Villa Park is a very different beast to that of more than 50 years ago. The Holte End was initially covered in 1962 and this was replaced as recently as 1990, but this cover was short-lived and the end was demolished in May 1994; the new Holte Stand was completed in the following December. The new Holte End facade adopted a red-brick style in keeping with the listed Trinity Road facade. Opposite the Trinity Road Stand, the Witton Lane Stand was rebuilt in 1993; now known as the Doug Ellis Stand, the structure was opened in January 1994 and cost some £5 million. The Witton End was replaced by a new North Stand in 1997, which took Villa Park's capacity to just over 39,000. The next phase in the club's scheme to produce a ground with a 50,000-seat capacity came in mid-2000 with the demolition of the listed and attractive Trinity Road Stand and the construction of a new three-tier structure that overhangs, in part, Trinity Road. This took Villa Park's capacity to almost 43,000 and, with the demise of Wembley Stadium, the ground played host to an England international. The next phase of the ground's redevelopment will be a further extension to the North Stand, which will see the capacity increase to some 50,000, although there is currently no time-scale for this work.

Below: 1951 (R15969)
Right: 2004 (697429)

Barnsley

Then: 10 October 1952
Now: 15 June 2004

It was in 1887 that Barnsley St Peters was founded — the 'St Peters' was dropped a decade later — and the team played its first game at Oakwell on 8 September 1888. In 1895 the first — and short-lived — stand was constructed and, three years later, in 1898 Barnsley joined the Second Division of the Football League. The central section of the Main Stand — later extended — was built in 1904. The ground as illustrated in the first of these two photographs was in transition. The Pontefract End was covered in the late 1940s, whilst the extension of the terracing along the Popular Side was not completed until 1954. The changes that have occurred over the past 50 years have been dramatic as Oakwell was converted into an all-seater stadium with a modern capacity of 19,000. Although the Main Stand is still extant, even this structure has been much modified (with seating inserted in the Paddock in front of it; this took place in 1995). The first stage of the development was the construction of a small facility for the disabled between the Main Stand and the Kop; this, which was the first purpose-built accommodation for disabled fans in British football, was completed in 1982. Four years later a new control room was completed and in 1989 the original 1962 floodlighting was replaced. The two major developments — the two-tier East Stand (7,200 seats costing £2.65 million) and the South Stand (which cost £2 million) — were opened in March 1993 and August 1995 respectively. Seats were inserted on the still open Kop in 1994 and the area allocated to away fans. With the completion of the South Stand, the club turned its attention to the reconstruction of the Kop. The new North Stand, with its 6,000-seater capacity, was completed in 1999. This work took the capacity at Oakwell to 23,000. The next phase for the ground's redevelopment will be the reconstruction of the old West Stand and open (but seated) paddock, although there is no confirmed schedule for this work currently and the club's current League One status means that there is no great urgency to undertake the work.

Right: 1952 (A47420)
Far Right: 2004 (697503)

Birmingham City

Then: 12 June 1967
Now: 1999

In an age when football is increasingly dominated by colourful and high-profile chairmen, few come more colourful than David Sullivan, who arrived at Birmingham City in January 1993 bringing with him Karren Brady (who was soon to be installed as the club's new Managing Director). For City fans, used to strange goings-on, the arrival of a chairman whose fortune had been made through another sort of 'blue' was probably to be expected; however, under Sullivan's control the ground has improved dramatically over the past decade.

Founded as Small Heath Alliance in 1875, the future Birmingham City — the club became Birmingham FC in the first decade of the 20th century and Birmingham City after World War 2 — played its first game at St Andrews on 26 December 1906. The ground, developed by an unknown (Harry Pumphrey) as opposed to Archibald Leitch at rivals Aston Villa, then consisted of a Main Stand and terracing along the Coventry Road side. The first of these two photographs illustrates the ground as it existed before the requirements of safety legislation brought changes. The original Main Stand was destroyed by fire in January 1942 and the structure illustrated here dated from the early 1950s. The Kop — the Coventry Road side — had been reroofed in 1947. The Tilton Road End had been covered in the late 1950s, shortly after floodlighting had been installed in 1956. The last section of the old St Andrews to be covered was the Railway End, where a two-tier stand was erected in 1963-4.

Work started on the redevelopment of St Andrews in the early 1990s and the Coventry Road side and the Tilton End have been replaced with new stands; the original structures were demolished in April 1994 and the new stands were opened on 15 November 1994. The next phase of the work was the reconstruction of the old Railway End, which commenced in 1998 and which opened on 31 January 1999. The new stand has a capacity of over 8,000, taking St Andrews' current capacity to just over 30,000. The only remaining section of the old ground is the Main Stand, although the club has plans — with no confirmed time scale — for the replacement of this with a new 7,500-seat stand, taking the ground's capacity to 36,500.

Inset: 1999 (679479)
Right: 1967 (A172543)

Blackburn Rovers

Then: 19 October 1928
Now: 1 March 2002

One of the most radical transformations of any league grounds in recent years is that at Ewood Park, home of Blackburn Rovers. Although the club, founded in November 1875, had played there earlier, Ewood Park was to become the team's permanent home only in 1890, with the club playing its first game there on 13 September of that year. The 'Then' shot shows well the state of the ground in the late 1920s; the most dramatic feature is the brand-new roof over the Riverside Stand, which was reroofed in 1928 (the year of the photograph). The Riverside Stand had originally been roofed in 1913. Opposite the Riverside Stand is the Main (or Nuttall Street) Stand, which was constructed in 1906 and officially opened on 1 January 1907. The angle was the result of following the line of the road. The covered Darwen End — with the Fernhurst Mill beyond — received its roof in 1905 and the terrace was concreted over two years later. The fourth side of the ground was the uncovered Blackburn End, which was concreted in 1928; this end was not to receive a cover until 1960. Today all four sides of the ground have changed out of all recognition. The first change occurred after the Riverside Stand was condemned in 1985; the then club chairman persuaded Walkersteel to support the construction of a new stand — the Walkersteel Stand — which opened in 1988; it received seating in 1990. Following Walkersteel's multi-million pound sale, Jack Walker bought the club in early 1991 and some 18 months later the club with his

millions behind it announced that Ewood Park would be rebuilt. There was opposition, not least from the residents of Nuttall Street and from those destined to lose their jobs with the closure and demolition of Fernhurst Mill. In the event, the original proposals for a 25,000 all-seater stadium were amended to take the capacity to more than 30,000 and in December 1992 work commenced with the demolition of houses along Nuttall Street. In March 1993 the old Darwen End was demolished; the new stand opened in two stages in August and October the same year. In May 1993, the Blackburn Road End was cleared; the new stand opened in two stages in November 1993 and February 1994. Whilst this work was being completed, the old Main Stand was demolished; it re-opened in August and November 1994. Today, Ewood Park has a capacity of 31,367; future plans envisage the redevelopment of the Riverside Stand to take capacity to 40,000, although there is no schedule for this work at the current time.

Below: 1928 (25178)
Right: 2002 (692612)

Blackpool

Then: 20 September 1951
Now: 23 February 2004

For many years Blackpool was one of the most glamorous football clubs in Britain, but it and Bloomfield Road had fallen on hard times. Blackpool was founded in 1887 and, between 1896 and 1899, was a member of the Football League; in December 1899 it merged with South Shore, which had played its first game at the future Bloomfield Road on 21 October 1899. The newly-united Blackpool was readmitted to the League in 1900. The 'Then' photograph shows Bloomfield Road in 1951 when Blackpool was at its peak as a footballing team. Parallel to the railway lines is the West Stand, which had been built in 1917 to replace an earlier structure destroyed by fire. The South Stand was built in 1925; clearly visible in this photograph is the short balcony-like structure that linked the South and West stands. In 1930, the short Motor Stand at the North End was moved to form an angled structure between the existing West Stand and the newly-built Kop. Also in 1930, a roof was fitted over part of the East Terrace.

The first edition of this book, published in 1998, commented that little had changed at Bloomfield Road over the past 50 years, although the club had plans — complicated by the gaoling of chairman Owen Oyston — for either redevelopment or relocation. The cover over the east side of the ground had been extended but, until the summer of 2000, little else had happened. However, with the club now committed to redevelopment at Bloomfield Road, the old Kop and West Stand were demolished, giving the club a capacity of only just over 6,000 for the 2000/01 season. Work on the replacement structures in this £10.7 million project did not start until towards the end of the season and the new North and West stands opened in February 2002. With this phase of the rebuilding concluded, attention turned to the South Stand and East Terrace, both of which were demolished in mid-2003. The latter was replaced by a temporary, open, stand seating 1,700 and used for away fans; whilst the redevelopment of the South Stand is currently in abeyance. Once the new South Stand is completed, the redevelopment will be completed by a new permanent East Stand, providing seated accommodation for 16,000 in total.

Left: 1951 (A39906)
Below: 2004 (697003)

Bolton Wanderers

Then: 20 September 1971
Now: 1 May 2001

Founded in 1874 and becoming Bolton Wanderers three years later, the club moved to Burnden Park in 1895, playing its first game there on 11 September of that year. The 'Then' view, taken in 1971, shows well the nature of Burnden Park before the club's declining fortunes (both financially and on the pitch) forced the sale of part of the Railway End Terrace in the early 1980s and the consequent building of a supermarket on the site (in 1986). The Railway End as illustrated here was the result of modifications undertaken in 1947 after one of English football's less well known tragedies, when, on 9 March 1946, 33 were crushed to death. The Main Stand was constructed in 1904, whilst the angled extension was completed in 1915. Opposite the Main Stand, and closest to the camera, is the Burnden Stand, which replaced the earlier Darcy Lever Stand (of 1895) in 1928. The fourth side is the Great Lever End; this was terraced and provided with a roof in 1906. Floodlights were installed originally in 1957. In the early 1990s detailed proposals for the club to relocate were first formulated and, in December 1995, work started on a new stadium near Horwich. The 1996/97 season was the last that Bolton played at Burnden Park and the new Reebok Stadium was inaugurated, with the club having regained its position in the Premiership, at the start of the 1997/98 season. The new ground, ideally placed for road and rail services, now has a capacity of 27,800, all-seated. Access to the ground has been improved by the opening of a new railway station — Horwich Parkway — slightly to the west of the stadium. Following relegation at the end of 1997/98, Wanderers returned to the First Division. A successful campaign in 2000/01, however, saw the team return to the Premiership; ironically, however, such is the pace of ground redevelopment that the Reebok Stadium is now one of the smaller-capacity grounds in the Premiership and, whilst the team now seems to have consolidated its Premiership position, the size of the ground may yet prove a weakness.

Right: 2001 (688302)
Far Right: 1971 (A216922)

Boston United

Then: 1967
Now: 2003

Promoted to the Football League at the start of the 2002/03 season, Boston United have been based at York Street (or Shodfriars Lane as it is sometimes known) for 70 years, although the club's history stretches back to the late 19th century when two pub-based teams were established in the town. The club was reformed in the early 1930s, by which date the ground already possessed rudimentary facilities at the Town End. The 1930s saw the construction of a wooden stand with paddock; opposite was the Spayne Road side which was an open terrace initially. In 1955 the York Street Stand was constructed and floodlightling was also installed in the mid-1950s. In the late 1970s, the club missed out on promotion to the Football League and, as a result, action was taken to raise the standard of the ground to meet League criteria. Work started in 1978 with the construction of the Spayne Road Stand and the covering of the Town End Terrace. A new Main Stand — now called the Finnforest Stand — was built in 1981. Replacement floodlighting was also installed as were turnstiles. Today, York Street has a capacity of 6,643 although it is probable that the club will follow the current trend and look to relocate; whilst nothing has been confirmed as yet, it is expected that an announcement over the ground's future will be made in late 2004.

Left: 1967 (A172717)
Above: 2003 (693094)

Bournemouth

Then: 17 May 1939
Now: 28 May 2003

Following its rescue during the summer of 1997, AFC Bournemouth — the title the club adopted in 1971 — became Britain's first community football club.

The future AFC Bournemouth was founded as Boscombe St Johns in 1890; it became Boscombe FC in 1899 and played its first game at Dean Court on 31 December 1910. The ground as illustrated in the 'Then' shot dates from the era after the club's election to the Football League — as Bournemouth & Boscombe Athletic — in 1923. Opened officially on 27 August 1927, the Main Stand used materials salvaged from the Empire Exhibition at Wembley. This was followed in September 1936 by the cover over the South End terrace; this is the structure that looks new in the photograph. The ground continued to evolve over the next 60 years. The West Terrace was covered completely in 1957 and was known as the New Stand. Floodlighting was installed in 1961 and in 1992 the old Main Stand was reclad and provided with new seats and a small number of executive boxes. By the 2000/01 season, Dean Court's capacity was 10,770, of which 3,141 were seated.

For a number of years there was debate about either reconstruction at Dean Court or relocation, with a site identified alongside the A338 Wessex Way. In the event, despite concerns about Dean Court's location and access, the former solution was adopted and the old Dean Court bade farewell to football at the end of the 2000/01 season. The entire stadium was demolished at the end of the season, with the ground's axis being swung round 90° for the new ground. Work progressed rapidly during the course of the close season and the new ground was due to open early in the 2001/02 season. As a result of League dispensation, Bournemouth played its first games of that season at Dorchester Town's ground as the new Dean Court was not yet finished. The first game at the new stadium, with its 9,600 all-seated capacity, was on 10 November 2001. The club has plans, but no confirmed timescale at present, to construct the fourth side of the ground.

Left: 1939 (PR2704)

Above: 2003 (695751)

Bradford City

Then: 7 May 1966
Now: 1 March 2002

Few football fans will ever to be able to forget the horrors of 11 May 1985 when, instead of celebrating winning the Third Division title, 56 fans were killed when Valley Parade's Main Stand caught fire. Much of the redevelopment work that has changed the face of football in Britain was the result of safety checks after the fire. Much has been written about the causes of the fire elsewhere and further discussion would be inappropriate here.

Bradford City AFC was formed in 1903 out of an earlier club — Manningham — which had been one of the founder members of the breakaway Northern Rugby Union (the later Rugby League) — and played its first game at Valley Parade on 5 September 1903. The ground originally dated from the 1880s. So keen was the Football League to see football grow in one of the traditional heartlands of rugby, that the team was admitted immediately to the Football League and such was the success of the team that First Division football and the FA Cup (in 1911) were both soon achieved. As football prospered, so the ground was improved with much of the work being undertaken in 1908-9 by Archibald Leitch. The ground, as illustrated in the 'Then' shot, was very much his work; he designed the ill-fated Main Stand and the Manningham (Nunn's Kop) End. On the Midland Road side he designed a second stand; however, the foundations of this structure were found to be unsafe in 1949 and the frame was sold to Berwick Rangers in 1951. The 'Then' view shows Valley Parade at an interesting stage of its development. In 1954 a new Midland Road side was constructed, but this lasted only until 1960. In 1966 the pitch was moved closer to the Main Stand; this released a narrow strip of land upon which a new Midland Road Side was constructed. This work is that shown underway in this photograph. Subsequent to the photograph, in 1970, seating was installed in the Main Stand Paddock.

Following the fire, Bradford City was forced to play its games for a season at Elland Road, Leeds Road and Odsal. The opportunity of relocating from Valley Parade was one that never was really a possibility and, on 14 December 1986, the new Valley Parade was unveiled in a friendly between City and a England Select XI. As reconstructed, the new ground consisted of a new Main Stand, and a covered Kop, with the original Bradford End and Midland Road Side left intact. The Bradford End was rebuilt in 1991 and a brand new Midland Road Stand was built in 1996; this structure was officially opened by HM the Queen when she visited the city on 27 March 1997 to present the Maundy Money at Bradford Cathedral. This took Valley Parade's capacity to 18,018, of which 10,748 were seated. However, time was running out for the Kop and, during the summer of 1999, the structure was replaced by a massive new stand — the Carlsberg Stand. The work, when completed, took the ground's capacity to 18,276 and was marked by City's promotion — for the first time since 1922 — to the top flight of English football. Under the ambitious chairmanship of Geoffrey Richmond, further redevelopment commenced during the summer of 2000, with the conversion of the 1986-built Main (Sunwin) Stand to a new two-tier structure and the building of a corner stand between the Sunwin and Carlsberg Stands; this work took place during the 2000/01 season and took Valley Parade's capacity to 25,136 on completion. However, the end of the 2000/01 season was marked by the club's relegation to the First Division and further plans — which envisaged the expansion of the Midland Road (CIBA) Stand — to take the ground's capacity to more than 30,000 are unlikely to be progressed in the foreseeable future given the club's well-publicised financial problems and relegation, at the end of 2003/04, to the League One.

Right: 1966 (A161386)
Inset: 2002 (692548)

Brentford

Then: 1 July 1957
Now: 16 June 2003

Although Brentford was founded in 1889, it was not until 1904 that the club moved to Griffin Park, playing its first game there on 1 September of that year. In 1920 the club joined the Third Division of the Football League and it is from this period, and the club's remarkable rise to the First Division by the early 1930s, that the ground as illustrated in the 1957 photograph dates. In 1927 a new Main Stand was constructed. This was followed in 1931 by the installation of a cover over the New Road Terrace (opposite the Main Stand). The Brook Road End was roofed in two stages in 1933 and 1935 whilst in the latter year seating was installed in the wings adjacent to the Main Stand. Apart from this, the only major change to be recorded prior to the date of the 'Then' photograph was the installation of floodlights in 1954. The more recent photograph shows that there have been some considerable changes over the past 40 years. In February 1983, part of the Main Stand was destroyed by fire; the rebuilt section — distinguishable because of the changed roofline — was reopened at the start of the 1984/85 season. Following the Bradford City fire, the ground's capacity was reduced to 9,500 and the ground was under further threat after the Taylor Report, when the capacity of the Ealing Terrace was reduced to only 793 from 4,000. The club was faced with the fact that it occupies a confined space with little scope for development, but tentative plans for relocation in the late 1980s came to nothing. Thus the ground soldiers on, although there remain new plans for relocation in the long term.

Under the chairmanship of Ron Noades, the club had expressed interest — as have other clubs — in the site of the Feltham Arena, where a new 15,000-seat stadium could be constructed. The future is, however, uncertain — with Noades no longer chairman but still the owner of the ground — and there have been rumours of possible ground-sharing with either Woking or Kingstonian. The current plan favoured by the club is relocation to a new 25,000-seat stadium close to Kew Bridge, although there is no confirmed timescale at present.

Apart from the Main Stand, other significant changes included the sale of land behind the Brook Road Terrace in 1985 and this sale generated the funds to enable the building of the small two-tier structure; this opened in late 1986. Also in 1986, the rear section of the New Road Terrace was dismantled and the roof cut back; this area has subsequently had seating fitted. In 1991/92 the seating in the Main Stand was increased. The Ealing Terrace has had work undertaken on it in order to increase capacity, but plans for the construction of a new stand were rejected by Hounslow Council following objections from local residents. One other major difference over the past 40 years — the club takes advantage of its location on the flightpath into Heathrow to sell advertising space on the roof of the Main Stand and the New Road Terrace.

Below: 1957 (A68145)
Right: 2003 (695941)

26

Brighton & Hove Albion

Then: 23 April 1972
Now: 28 May 2003

The story of Brighton & Hove Albion, certainly over the past decade, is not a happy one, although the fact that the club has now been able to return to Sussex after a year's exile at Gillingham holds out some prospect of a rosier future. The first club to play at the Goldstone Ground was Hove FC, which played its first game there on 7 September 1901. Ironically, it was this same month which saw the earlier Brighton & Hove Rangers change their name to Brighton & Hove Albion; in February 1902, Albion, which had been playing elsewhere, discovered that they were unable to fulfil a fixture at their existing ground and Hove offered them the opportunity of playing at the Goldstone Ground. Eventually in 1904, Albion, after sharing the Goldstone with Hove for two years, took over the lease and began a period of occupation which was to last 93 years. The club was to become a member of the Third Division of the Football League in 1920. The 'Then' photograph shows the ground in the period just before the club's one brief sojourn in the First Division (1979-83). The South and North Ends had been covered some time; the former from the 1930s. On the west side, the West Stand was constructed in 1958 when the club achieved its first ever promotion. It was never more than two-thirds full length and, in the period of the club's run in the First Division, a temporary 974-seat stand — known popularly as the Lego Stand — was constructed between it and the North End. Although the 'Now' photograph shows the temporary ground at Withdean — ironically one of the earlier Brighton clubs played for a period at Withdean — it is worth relating the changes that occurred at the Goldstone between 1972 and the club's controversial departure in May 1997. In 1979 the roof over the North End was dismantled; it was replaced in 1985 at a cost of £1.2 million. In 1980 the South End was damaged by fire; it was repaired and seating was installed. The East Terrace was never covered; one of the restrictions in the club's ownership was that no structure of more than 50ft in height could be constructed on this side. The story of Brighton's tribulations at the Goldstone have been well recorded elsewhere; suffice to record here is the fact that a combination of rising debt and an inability to relocate saw the ground sold and the club forced to groundshare from May 1997 onwards. The summer 1997 close season saw the club variously linked with sites in Brighton itself and at either Millwall or Gillingham; in the event the Seagulls played their 'home' games at Gillingham during 1997/98.

At the start of the 1998/99 season the team returned to Brighton, playing its home games at the Withdean Stadium where stands were constructed on the north and south sides. This gives the ground a capacity of some 7,000, although the stadium is very much a temporary measure since the club intends to build a brand-new stadium at Village Way North, Falmer. This new ground, with a planned capacity of 22,000 all-seated and costing £44 million, has proved controversial and the club awaited a final decision from the Deputy Prime Minister, John Prescott. In late July it was announced that the Government had decided to refer the application back in order to examine the possibility of alternative locations. At the very least, the club will be based at Withdean for probably a couple of seasons and, as a temporary measure, it is looking at increasing capacity at Withdean by 2,000.

Below: 1972 (A228235)
Right : 2003 (695791)

Bristol City

Then: 18 April 1967
Now: 14 February 2002

A number of professional clubs were established in Bristol at the end of the 19th century; these included Bristol City and Bedminster. It was the latter which used Ashton Gate for home games, playing their first game there on 12 September 1896. In 1900 Bristol City and Bedminster merged and, in the following year, joined the Football League. From 1901 the merged club used the old Bristol City ground, but in 1904 the club moved back to Ashton Gate, playing its first game there on 27 August 1904. Although the new occupants undertook some work at the ground — including a relocation of the pitch — the view visible in the 'Then' shot is the result of development work from the 1920s onwards. In 1928 the Winterstoke End was roofed; this long structure is much wider than normal structures at the ends and implies that, perhaps, the club was contemplating a realignment of the pitch. In the event this did not occur. The Main Stand — known as the Grandstand and since 1992 called after ex-chairman Des Williams — was constructed in 1951-3, following the destruction of the earlier stand during the Blitz of January 1941. Opposite the Main Stand stood, until 1966, a structure known as the Cowshed; this formed part of the surviving cover along this side, the bulk of which had been destroyed by fire in 1929.

As can be seen, the changes at Ashton Gate appear to be radical; however, they are not quite as dramatic as they seem. In 1970, the old Cowshed area was replaced by a new structure, named after Harry Dolman, who had been chairman of the club in the early 1950s. After the Taylor Report, considerable work was undertaken from 1991. This included the installation of seats in the Grandstand Paddock and in the Winterstoke End. In addition, the existing three structures — the Grandstand, the Dolman Stand and the Winterstoke End — were all reclad in red and white panels. At the same time, the roof of the Grandstand was extended over the seats installed in the Paddock. Finally, in August 1994, the £1.8 million North Stand was opened to replace the existing open Ashton Road End. This, complete with 4,190 seats, was a much smaller structure than the two-tiered stand originally proposed but which was successfully opposed by local residents. Today, Ashton Gate has a capacity of 21,200.

When the last edition of this book was published there were plans — but no definite time-scale — for the possible redevelopment of the Brunel Williams Stand into a new 12,000-seat structure or, alternatively, for the club to relocate to a brand-new 36,000-seat ground at Hengrove Park. However, in November 2002 it was announced that the council was withdrawing from the scheme to build a new stadium for the city, leaving City to develop plans to rebuild Ashton Gate. Planning permission has been granted to rebuild the Wedlock, Williams and Dolman stands — in that order — to take capacity to 30,000 ultimately. Whilst it was expected that work would start during 2004, nothing had occurred by the time that this edition was being prepared.

Left: 1967 (A170622)
Below: 2002 (692238)

Bristol Rovers

Then: 18 April 1967
Now: 14 February 2002

Another of the sadly nomadic football clubs, Rovers were exiled from their native city for a decade following their departure from Eastville in April 1986. The club was established as the bizarrely named Black Arabs in 1883, not becoming Bristol Eastville Rovers until 1897; the Eastville was dropped in 1898. The reason for the change of name was the fact that the club had acquired Eastville in 1897 and on 3 April of that year played its first game there. The existing ground had included a 500-seat South Stand and the ground was further developed. The scene as illustrated in the 'Then' photograph results largely from the period after 1920 when Rovers were elected to the Football League. In 1924 the South Stand was completed. This was followed, in the early 1930s, by a decision which was to have a dramatic impact on the future of the club — the construction of a greyhound racing track. This work, which opened in July 1932, required the end terraces to be moved back from the pitch. More significantly, however, in 1940 ownership of the ground was transferred to the greyhound racing company; thereafter, Rovers were simply to lease the stadium. This was ultimately to lead to Rovers' departure in the mid-1980s. Also featured in the photograph of Eastville is the North Stand, which was constructed in 1958, and the cover over the West Terrace, which was added in 1961. In 1959, floodlighting was installed.

The sorry saga of Rovers — or the Gasheads as the team was nicknamed as a result of the slightly less than salubrious surroundings that the club occupied — began to unravel in 1979 when the lease expired. This uncertainty was followed on 16 August 1980 by the destruction of the South Stand by fire; for a period Rovers shared Ashton Gate, but the prospect of both Bristol clubs sharing in the long term were scuppered by City's financial problems. In the event Rovers returned to Eastville until the final farewell on 26 April 1986. From then, until the end of the 1995/96 season, the club played at Bath City's Twerton Park, before returning to Bristol and groundsharing with Bristol RUFC at the Memorial Ground. The 'Now' photograph illustrates the Memorial Ground, with the structures installed to accommodate both Rovers and the new professional era in Rugby Union, most recently stands at both Blackthorn and South ends in 1999/2000. The ground's capacity today is 11,917 although Rovers' long-term plans envisaged the construction of their own stadium in the city. However, in a reversal of fortunes, the tenant became the owner as financial problems at the rugby club lead Rovers to take-over the ownership of the site. Future developments see the ground's capacity being increased ultimately to 20,000 through the replacement of the Centenary Stand and Terrace and the South Stand, although there is no time-scale at present.

Below: 2002 (692203)
Right: 1967 (A170596)

Burnley

Then: 18 July 1961
Now: 23 February 2004

With a population of only some 75,000, Burnley is the smallest town in England to have sustained First Division football for any length of time and, with the relocation of Stoke City to the new Britannia Ground, only Preston North End can claim to have played continuously at the same ground for longer. Formed in 1881 as Burnley Rovers Rugby Club, football was adopted in May 1882 and, on 17 February 1883 the club played its first game at Turf Moor. As illustrated in the first of these photographs, which predates the era of the colourful chairman Bob Lord who did much to upgrade Turf Moor, the ground was covered on three sides, the exception being the Bee Hole End closest to the camera. To the left of the Bee Hole End is the Main (Brunshaw Road) Stand; this structure dated back to 1908. Opposite the Main Stand is the Longside; the cover illustrated here had been installed in 1954. The Cricket Field End was covered in 1909. Finally, floodlighting was installed in 1957.

Over the past 30 years all four sides at Turf Moor have been redeveloped. The first change occurred between 1967 and 1969 when the old Cricket Field End was replaced by a new stand; this was officially opened by the then Prime Minister some four years after it was completed. In 1974 Edward Heath, by this time leader of the opposition, opened the new Main Stand; this was now named after Bob Lord. For the next 20 years Turf Moor was to be a contrast; half the ground had been rebuilt, but the remainder was largely unchanged from that pictured in 1961. However, in September 1995 contracts were let for the £5.2 million construction of replacement Bee Hole and Longside stands. Work on these structures started in September 1995 and work was completed the following year. Today, Turf Moor has an all-seater capacity of 22,500; any future development work will occur at the Cricket Field (Endsleigh) End. However, this will require the cricket club to be relocated in order to construct a 7,000-seat two-tiered stand and, in the event that plan fails, attention will turn to the Bob Lord Stand.

Above: 1961 (A93606)
Right: 2004 (696996)

34

Bury

Then: August 1935
Now: 23 February 2004

The Shakers — as Bury are nicknamed — were formed in April 1885 and played their first game at Gigg Lane on 6 June 1885. The club joined the Football League in 1895. The 'Then' photograph shows the ground immediately prior to the building of the Manchester Road Stand in 1938. The ground as illustrated here was largely the result of reconstruction work in the 1920s. In 1922 the end terraces had been rebuilt, followed two years later by the building of a new Main Stand and the fitting of 2,000 seats into the South Stand (a building which dated from 1906 and which had replaced a structure dating from 1887). Also dating from 1924 was the small area known as the Boys' Stand alongside the South Stand; this was roofed in 1926. Today the ground has been much altered as can be seen from the more recent photograph. The Boys' Stand was demolished in 1985 and part of the site used in 1995 for the construction of a new ground control room. Also in 1985 part of the Manchester Road End was also taken out of use. The Main Stand was reconstructed in 1992. The South Stand was rebuilt in 1994 and was followed in 1995 by the construction of the Manchester Road Stand. Also in 1995 came the replacement of the existing floodlights and some limited work at the Cemetery End.

The final stage in the redevelopment of Gigg Lane was the rebuilding of the Cemetery End in 1999-2000. This took the ground's capacity, all-seated, to 12,500.

Below: 1935 (C19898)
Left: 2004 (696982)

Cambridge United

Then: 26 May 1933
Now: 26 May 2003

Founded as Abbey United in 1912 and not becoming Cambridge United until 1951, United joined the Football League in 1970 when the team was elected to the Fourth Division in place of Bradford (Park Avenue). The first of these two photographs shows how rudimentary the facilities were at the ground in the period immediately after the club moved there in 1932; the first game was played at the Abbey Stadium on 31 August 1932, but it was not until 1934 that the first, wooden, stand was erected. The land for the ground, located to the west of the allotments was provided by the club's president Henry Clement Francis. Although the club was offered more land, it declined the offer with the result that once the club moved up the Football League — and by the late 1970s it had reached the upper echelons of the Second Division (before relegation saw it back temporarily in the Third — old Fourth — Division) — there were problems with trying to improve facilities. The more recent photograph shows the ground as it existed at the end of the 2002/03 season. The Main Stand is on the east side; this was initially constructed in 1967 and doubled in length in 1980; the extension is known as the Biley Stand after the player whose sale helped to fund the development. Opposite is the Habbin Stand; this was constructed in 1960 and, in 1980, was partially fitted with seats. Other covered accommodation is the 40yd-long roof over part of the Newmarket Road (North) End.

Work started on the redevelopment of the ground at the end of the 2000/01 season and saw the demolition of the uncovered South Terrace. The £4.2 million scheme envisaged moving the pitch towards the south and building a new 1,524-seat South Stand over part of the adjacent allotments. The space created at the north end allowed for the building of a new 4,000 seat North Stand. However, the planned demolition of the North Terrace did not take place resulting in the South Stand, completed in 2002, remaining some 15m from the playing area. Once funds are available, the club intends to rebuild the North Terrace into a 3,500-seat stand complete with 14 executive boxes. This will be followed by the construction of a new 4,000-seat Main Stand and, finally, by the rebuilding of the Habbin Stand. It is the club's intention to retain standing accommodation at the ground for as long as the League will permit but the stadium will ultimately have a 10,000 all-seated capacity.

Left: 2003 (695784)
Below: 1933 (41310)

Cardiff City

Then: 11 June 1974
Now: 30 April 2001

League football was a relatively late arrival in South Wales, although Cardiff City's progress once admitted to the Football League in 1920 was swift, culminating in winning the FA Cup in 1927 — the only occasion that the trophy has been won by a non-English team. The club itself was founded in 1899 and first played at Ninian Park on 1 September 1910. The ground as illustrated in the 'Then' shot shows the state of Ninian Park in the early 1970s. The Main Stand is on the left side. The bulk of the stand dated to 1937 when the original structure was burnt down; the Main Stand was extended in 1972-3. Opposite the Main Stand is the Popular Side (or 'Bob Bank'); this was increased in size in 1958 with the roof over the rear section constructed in 1958. The Canton Stand (at the north end) was constructed in 1920, whilst the roof over the Grangetown End was constructed in 1928. Floodlights were installed in 1960. The more recent shot illustrates well the changes that have occurred at Ninian Park over the past quarter of a century. Once one of the venues used by the Welsh national side, the fact that Ninian Park is not all-seater has meant that internationals are no longer played here. In the mid-1970s, the Safety of Sports Grounds Act cut the ground's capacity from 46,000 to 10,000 although this was later increased once work had been undertaken. Further restrictions resulted after the Bradford fire and today Ninian Park's capacity is less than 15,000. Changes to the ground started in 1977 when the roof of the Grangetown End was demolished and the bank reduced. For a period from 1990 until 1992 this end was completely disused. Opposite, the Canton Stand was refurbished in 1992 and seats were added in part; the rear of the stand is out of use and hidden by a screen. The Main Stand paddock was fitted with seats in 1991 and the following year this section was covered by an extension to the existing roof. Also in 1992, seats were installed in the covered section of the Bob Bank whilst in 1993 the open terrace in front of this stand was taken out of use.

Ninian Park is increasingly careworn and, under the ambitious new chairman Sam Hammam (ex-supremo at Wimbledon), the club has plans for relocation. In the meantime some remedial work was undertaken at Ninian Park; this included the addition of seating to the Popular Bank and the roofing of the Grange End Terrace in 2001. Planning approval was given in December 2003 for the construction of the stadium, to be built at Leckwith close to the existing ground. The new stadium, costing £100 million and linked to a retail development, will initially provide accommodation for 30,000 but up to 60,000 eventually. Work is scheduled to start in August 2004 with a planned completion date of the start of the 2005/06 season.

Right: 1974 (AC278892)
Far right: 2001 (688026)

Charlton Athletic

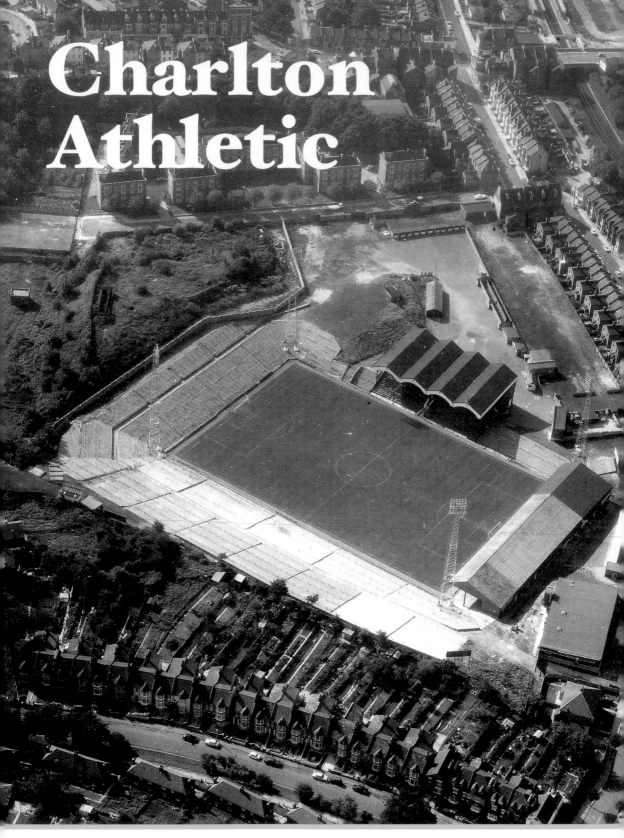

Then: 20 September 1970
Now: 18 February 2002

Few sagas in the history of English football have been more dramatic than the campaign waged by supporters of Charlton Athletic to see the club return to The Valley after its controversial departure after the game on 21 September 1985. Although The Valley could lay claim to being probably, in capacity terms, the largest ground in the Football League, the actual facilities offered remained poor. Charlton Athletic itself was formed in 1905, but did not play its first game at The Valley until 13 September 1919. Two years later the team entered the Football League. The ground as illustrated here shows the Main Stand with its four-span roof on the west side; this was constructed contemporaneously with the club's entry into the Football League. The only other covered accommodation was provided on the North Terrace, which was covered in 1934 (and damaged during the war). The huge East Terrace was completed during the 1930s, whilst in 1950 seats were installed in the Main Stand Paddock. Floodlighting was installed at The Valley in 1961.

Fifteen years after the date of the first photograph — on 21 September 1985 — the club left The Valley, to begin a seven-year period of exile initially at Crystal Palace and later at Upton Park. The campaign to see the team return to The Valley was long drawn out, highly political and eventually successful. The end result was that the team returned to The Valley in late 1992, playing its first game back there on 5 December 1992. In returning to The Valley the club was faced by many of the problems over the ground which had existed prior to its departure and which had remained unsolved during the club's absence. The changes to The Valley in the 30 years since the earlier photograph are evident. Of the ground that existed prior to the club's exile, only one element — the South Stand — is largely unchanged. The South (Jimmy Seed) Stand was opened in August 1981 replacing the original open terrace. The East Stand, which replaced the old East Terrace (the one part of the ground that could not be reopened in 1992 and which was demolished in 1993), was opened on 2 April 1994. The original Main (West) Stand roof had been replaced in 1979 and again a decade later; this structure, described as temporary, was to last almost a decade.

Work started at the Valley in early 1998 on the construction of a new West Stand; this was completed later that year and took the ground's capacity to fractionally over 20,000. In early 2001, following the granting of planning permission, work commenced on the construction of a new 6,500-seat North Stand as shown in the more recent photograph. This work, costing £9 million, was completed for the 2001/02 season and took the Valley's capacity to 26,500. Further planned work will see the ground's capacity increase ultimately to 40,000. This work will include the construction of a further tier on the East Stand and the complete rebuilding of the South Stand in two phases. There is, however, no timescale at present for this work.

Far left: 1970
(A208189)
Left: 2002 (692142)

Chelsea

Then: 1935
Now: 15 June 2004

Given the history of Stamford Bridge and of its relationship with Chelsea, it is perhaps appropriate that the ground shares — coincidentally, as in reality the name is derived from a local bridge — a name with an 11th century battle in Yorkshire. The battle of Stamford Bridge in 1066 was won by King Harold, who defeated the Vikings before losing his next European encounter with William the Conqueror at Hastings. Virtually throughout the history of Stamford Bridge, the ground's ownership has been distinct from that of the club with the result that, until recently, facilities were poor in comparison with other major grounds in the London area. Whilst Stamford Bridge may have hosted FA Cup finals between 1920 and 1922, it was gradually eclipsed by other stadia, such as Highbury, and no greater contrast can be noted than the fact that the 'Then' shot here postdates the Arsenal 'Then' (see page 7).

Stamford Bridge's sporting life started in 1877 as an athletics circuit — an activity that was to continue until 1932 — and it was not until 1905 that Chelsea was established to play football at the ground. Stamford Bridge saw its first football match on 4 September 1905; Chelsea were admitted at the start of the 1905/06 season to the Second Division of the Football League. The ground as illustrated in 1935 shows how relatively primitive the facilities were at the time, with the only covered accommodation being provided by the 1905 East Stand (designed by Archibald Leitch) and by the curious cover at the rear of the Fulham Road End. The latter, known as the Shed, was built in 1935 and was thus new at the time of the photograph. The fact that the ground's origins lay in an athletics circuit is evident; the track was also used for greyhound racing (until 1968) and for speedway (between 1928 and 1932).

Today Stamford Bridge has been radically rebuilt. The saga of the ground ownership and of the various roles of Ken Bates and the late Matthew Harding have been well documented elsewhere; suffice to note here that between 1983 and 1995 the future of both ground and club was in the balance. One factor in the emerging crisis was the cost of the new East Stand, which replaced the original Leitch structure (demolished in mid-1972) and which opened in August 1974; it was refurbished (including replacement seats) in the early 1990s. The ground has been largely redeveloped since 1993 under the concept of the 'Chelsea Village' which included plans for a hotel, flats, and underground car park as well as a 40,000-seat stadium. In order to accommodate all these elements, the pitch has been reduced in size and

the oval circuit has disappeared. Work started on the new North Stand in December 1993; the main section opened in November 1994 with the corner section at the northwest following in 1996. In the summer of 1994 the Shed was removed and the Fulham Road (South Bank) End modified to allow for temporary seating; work started on the underground car park behind the South Bank in 1995 and the new South Stand and associated hotel were constructed in 1996-7. Finally, in 1997, work started on the new West Stand. This work was long drawn out as — inevitably given the story of Chelsea — there was a dispute over the final form that the stand would take. By the late 1990s Stamford Bridge had a capacity of 35,629 which was due to rise to 42,000 once the final stage of the West Stand was completed.

However, planning disputes mean that the West Stand was destined to remain uncompleted for several seasons and it was only in 2000 that work recommenced on the completion of the stand. The impressive two-tier stand was completed during the course of the 2000/01 season and completes current redevelopment work on the actual stadium at Stamford Bridge and takes the ground's capacity to 42,449.

Below: 2004 (697392)
Right: 1935 (A128707)

Cheltenham Town

Then: 28 June 1972
Now: 6 May 2003

Promoted to the Third Division at the end of the 1998/99 season, Cheltenham Town represent one of a number of teams promoted from the Conference in recent seasons. The team was founded in 1892 and, after playing at Whaddon Road Lane and Carter's Field, moved to the current ground at Whaddon Road in 1932. The team joined the Southern League in 1935, where it remained until its first period in the future Conference in the mid-1980s. However, there was only a brief stay at this level, and the team was relegated back into the Southern League. A further promotion in 1996/97 brought the team back to the Conference and, despite being relatively unfancied, promotion to the Football League was secured in 1999.

The Victory Ground opened in 1927 under the aegis of Cheltenham Original Brewers — who passed the ground (with covenants) to the local council in the 1940s — and the club turned professional in 1933. The first of these two photographs shows the ground as it existed in the early 1970s. The ground's original wooden stand had been replaced by a new 1,200-seat stand (costing £25,000) in 1963. Floodlighting had originally been installed in 1950 but the installation illustrated here dated to replacement in 1960. Opposite the Main Stand was a covered terrace — the Chicken Run — and around the pitch was a wooden fence; both of these were to be damaged in the great gale of October 1987.

Today, the ground possesses the Main Stand, which was upgraded during the course of the 1999/00 season, the covered Wymans Road Terrace (which was completed in 1990 to replace the earlier structure), the open Whaddon Road End and the Prestbury End. The latter was originally open terracing, but the new Cheltenham & Gloucester Stand was completed for the start of the 2000/01 season. Future work at Whaddon Road will include the construction of a new £1 million 2,000-seat stand to replace the existing Wymans Road side. This project was due to be completed by the start of the 2001/02 season but has yet to be undertaken. When completed it will take the ground's capacity to 7,200.

Right: 1972 (A242970)
Above: 2003 (695567)

Chester City

Then: 1964
Now: 18 May 2004

For more than 80 years Chester City played at Sealand Road, illustrated on the right of the photograph below, until financial problems led to the club sharing Macclesfield Town's Moss Rose ground for two seasons between 1990 and 1992 before the club returned to its home city and the new Deva Stadium. When the ground was actually acquired by the club, in 1932 some 26 years after it started playing there, two sides of the ground were already covered: the Sealand Road Terrace was covered by a structure known as 'The Barn' and the Main Stand had been completed in April 1931. A short covered structure was later installed on the Popular Side; this was to be extended in 1968 shortly after the date of the 'Then' photograph. The floodlights, when recorded in 1964, were a relatively recent innovation, having been installed only in 1960. The fourth side of the ground, the Spion Kop, was never covered. One final modification to the ground was the construction of a new stand behind the existing Main Stand in 1979; on the completion of this new building the Main Stand illustrated in the 'Then' photograph was demolished. However, the pitch was not relocated closer to the new stand and there remained a considerable gap between pitch and stand until the final game at the ground on 28 April 1990. The story as to how the club came to lose Sealand Road and spend two years in exile is a long and complex one; suffice it here to note that Planning Permission was granted in late 1991 for the construction of a brand new stadium and work commenced on 28 January 1992. Work was rapid and the new ground was opened to League football on 25 August 1992. As constructed, the ground had a capacity of 6,000: 2,134 seated in the East (Main) Stand; 1,274 seated in the West Stand; and 1,296 standing on each of the covered terraces at the North and South ends. Unusually, the Main Stand is on the east; this is effectively the only part of the ground in England — the pitch and remaining stands are in Wales and, if the club's offices had been located on the west, it would have been forced to become a member of the Welsh, rather than English, FA.

Below: 1964 (A128707)
Left: 2004 (697201)

Chesterfield

Then: 7 August 1965
Now: 28 February 2002

The early history of Chesterfield and of the Saltergate ground are uncertain; suffice to note here that Chesterfield Town was founded in 1866 and played its first game at Saltergate in about 1880. Saltergate became the club's permanent home in 1887 and, from 1899 until 1909, Chesterfield Town played in the Football League. The club later became Chesterfield Municipal before becoming simply Chesterfield when rejoining the Football League in 1921. The 1965 shot shows the ground prior to the introduction of floodlights in 1967; Saltergate can claim the honour of being the last ground in the Football League to have permanent floodlighting installed. The Main Stand was opened on 7 November 1936. In the early 1950s the Compton Street cover opposite the Main Stand was extended the full length of the pitch, whilst in 1961 the Kop was covered. The fourth side, the Cross Street End, was (and remains) open terracing. As can be seen from the more recent photograph, little has changed at Saltergate over the past 37 years other than the arrival of the floodlighting. The ground, despite its antiquity, is confined and the club has, since the early 1990s, been examining the possibility of either redevelopment or relocation. One scheme was for the club to relocate to the former greyhound track at Wheeldon Park where a new 12,000-capacity stadium would have been constructed. Saltergate's current capacity is 8,000.

During the course of the 2000/01 season the position of Saltergate became increasingly tenuous. At one stage, the ground's capacity was threatened with a reduction to 2,600 as the Football Licensing Authority rejected the club's appeal to keep the terracing open. However, planning permission was granted on 21 May 2001 for the reconstruction of Saltergate as a 10,000-capacity all-seater stadium. Following the club's financial problems at the end of the 2000/01 season, a supporter's trust acquired the club. In early 2003, the trust balloted supporters as to whether to relocate or to rebuild; the decision was to support relocation and the club is now progressing with plans to move to the site of the old greyhound stadium at Brinington.

Far left: 1965 (A150330)
Left : 2002 (692592)

Colchester United

Then: 29 March 1968
Now: 17 May 2004

After its initial use by the army, the first football club to occupy Layer Road was the amateur team, Colchester Town (founded in 1873), which played its first game there on 4 November 1909. It was under Town's control that much of the work visible in the 1968 photograph was undertaken. The Main Stand was constructed on the south side of the pitch in 1932-3. This structure occupied the centre third of the side, with the remaining two thirds being occupied by terracing. Opposite, at the same time as the Main Stand was being built, a 50yd section of the Popular Side was being roofed; this became known as either the Cowshed or the Barn. In 1937, the professional team Colchester United was founded to replace Town and took over at Layer Road; the new occupants quickly moved to develop the ground further. A roof was built over the Layer Road End in 1937; this had to be replaced in 1938, whilst during World War 2 German POWs constructed wooden terracing beneath it. This wooden terracing was to survive until 1992, when it was rebuilt with concrete. Colchester United were admitted to the Football League in 1950 and in 1956-7 roofs were constructed over the terracing alongside the Main Stand. This was followed in 1959 by the installation of floodlights.

The 'Now' photograph shows the effects of a decade of change at Layer Road. In the immediate aftermath of the Bradford fire, capacity at the ground fell from 14,000 to 4,000 and, with the club's relegation to the Vauxhall Conference in 1990, crowds continued to shrink. A return to the Football League at the end of the 1991/92 season meant that the ground was now subject to the stringent requirements. Initial work included the concreting of the Layer Road Terrace. However, as the club initially wanted to relocate, other developments at Layer Road were low key. These have included the roofing of a further section of the Popular Side Terrace and its designation as a family area and, in 1995, the replacement of the

floodlights. Also in 1995, the west side of the ground — the Clock End — was reprofiled, a roof added and some 635 seats installed. Today, the ground's capacity is just under 8,000 but the club, following a feasibility study in early 1998, was uncertain as to whether it should further redevelop Layer Road or relocate. Consultants in early 1999 proposed relocation to a new 10,000-seat capacity stadium although it was some time before firm proposals were developed. Plans for the new ground — to be located close to the main A12 at Cuckoo Farm — were unveiled in mid-2001 and current plans are that the club will relocate for the start of the 2005/06 season.

Right: 2004 (697276)
Below: 1968 (A179262)

Coventry City

Then: 3 July 1972
Now: 30 April 2001

Of all the teams in the Premiership, there were few that had survived in the top flight for as long as Coventry City; each season, normally, brought a campaign against the much prophesied relegation, but each season the club somehow managed to survive until 2000/01. Highfield Road is very much a product, albeit updated, of the early days in the old First Division. The club's origins go back to 1883 when the team was established as the Singer Work's team; it became Coventry City in the early 1890s and played its first game at Highfield Road on 9 September 1899. Joining the Southern League in 1908, the team progressed to the Football League in 1919. The first of these two photographs shows work in progress in rerooofing the Thackhall Street (North) Stand; this originally dated back to 1910 but had been rebuilt in 1963-4 and became known as the Sky Blue Stand. Opposite the Thackhall Street Stand is the Main Stand; this had been destroyed by fire on 16 March 1968, but the replacement roof itself was destined to have a short life before itself being replaced. The 1968 Main Stand replaced one constructed in 1936, which itself replaced an older structure — the John Bull Stand — which dated back to 1899. The two-tier West Stand dated from 1967, when the club gained promotion to the First Division; this replaced an earlier structure, acquired from Twickenham, that had been erected in 1927. In 1972 the only open end of the ground was the Kop (East) Terrace, which had originally been built in 1922. During the late 1970s, Highfield Road became the first all-seater stadium in the Football League, but this was short-lived and by the mid-1980s standing accommodation was again provided. The more recent photograph shows the work that the club has undertaken over recent years in order to become again all-seater. Although the West Stand remains, opposite it is the East Stand, which was completed in August 1994. Also in 1994 the Sky Blue

Stand was rerooofed; this work has also been undertaken on the Main Stand. In 1995 all pre-1990 seats were replaced and, today, Highfield Road has an all-seater capacity of 23,662. Despite the expenditure of recent years, however, City announced in 1998 that it intended to follow the trend amongst larger clubs of seeking a larger capacity by relocating to a new ground. However, initial plans to have the ground available by the start of the 2002/03 season proved overly optimistic as work did not commence on the new 32,000-seat stadium until January 2004. The new stadium, scheduled to cost £113 million, is being built on the site of an old gasworks at Foleshill and will include a new railway station and retail development. The scheme is part funded by the local authority. Thus, the 2004/05 season will be City's last campaign at Highfield Road. The old stadium has already been sold and will be redeveloped once the club moves.

Below: 1972 (A235006)
Right: 2001 (688710)

Crewe Alexandra

Then: 26 April 1973
Now: 2000

With a capacity of just over 10,000, Gresty Road remains one of the smallest grounds in League One. Founded in the late 1870s, as the footballing section of the Alexandra Athletic Club, Crewe moved to Gresty Road in 1906. Although the club had been a founder member of the Second Division in 1892, it had failed to be re-elected in 1896 and it was not until 1921, when the club joined the new Third Division (North), that league football returned to the town. The ground as it is shown in the 'Then' photograph is very much the product of the era immediately after the club's return to the League. The major exception is the Main Stand; the original structure was burnt down in 1932 and was replaced by a new stand — which was opened on 5 November 1932. Floodlights were originally installed in 1958. More recent developments, reflected in the 'Now' photograph, are the construction of a Family Stand on the east (in 1992), the rebuilding of the open terrace at the Gresty Road End (in 1995) and the

refurbishment, with 1,680 seats installed on the old terrace, of the Popular Side (also in 1995). The biggest and most dramatic change to Gresty Road occurred at the end of the 1998/99 season, when it was announced that the old wooden Main Stand was to be demolished and replaced by a new 6,500-seat stand. The new Railtrack Stand was completed for the start of the 1999/00 season and gives the ground a highly unbalanced image. The next phase in the development of Gresty Road will feature the rebuilding of the Blue Bell BMW Stand as a two-tiered structure, although there is no timescale for this work.

Below: 1973 (655864)
Right: 2000 (684961)

Crystal Palace

Then: 1949
Now: 28 May 2003

Although based at Selhurst Park for more than 70 years, the origins of the club — as its name implies — go back to the famous Crystal Palace designed by Sir Joseph Paxton for the Great Exhibition of 1851. The present club, however, was only established in 1904 and, after an itinerant life, played its first game at the new Selhurst Park on 30 August 1924, having joined the Football League in 1920. At the time that the ground was opened, the facilities provided were an Archibald Leitch-designed Main Stand on the west and three sides of banking. As can be seen in the first of these two photographs, 25 years after the club moved to Selhurst Park the Main Stand remained the only covered accommodation although proper terracing had been installed along the lower sections of the other three sides of the ground. For the club's early years, these facilities, whilst rudimentary, probably sufficed; however, in the 1960s the club started an inexorable climb up the Football League and, by the end of the decade, had reached the old First Division. From the late 1960s onwards there have been significant developments at Selhurst Park. In addition to the physical changes at the ground, since 1985 Selhurst Park has also been shared by two other teams: Charlton Athletic from 1985 until 1991 and Wimbledon from 1992 to 2003. The more recent photograph shows the contemporary scene at Selhurst Park. The original 1924 stand remains, although it is

now all seater (with seating installed in its paddock in 1979 and with a hospitality suite built behind it in 1992-3). Opposite this is the Arthur Wait Stand (on the Park Road Side); this was initially built in 1969 and in 1990 was converted to an all-seater arrangement. The Whitehorse Lane (North) End was redeveloped in 1981; a reduced terrace was constructed with housing and a supermarket located behind. The Whitehorse Lane End was further modified in 1991 and 1992 by the addition of executive boxes and by being converted to an all-seater arrangement. The final development occurred in 1994-5 with the construction of the new Holmesdale Road Stand. The current capacity at Selhurst Park is 26,400; there are long terms plans for the redevelopment of the Main Stand (for which planning permission has been obtained), but there is no confirmed timetable at this stage and it is strongly opposed by local residents. If the club does not expand at Selhurst Park, then it may well seek to relocate. The situation at Selhurst Park is complicated by the fact that ownership of the ground is controlled by former club chairman, Ron Noades, whilst Palace itself is now controlled by Michael Jordan.

Left: 1949 (HAS/UK/49/217)
Below: 2003 (695768)

Darlington

Then: 15 May 1964
Now: 9 May 2003

The Quakers — as Darlington are nicknamed — were formed in September 1883 and were based from the start at Feethams, where cricket had been played since 1866. Many other football grounds were closely linked with cricket grounds — one can think immediately of Bradford (Park Avenue) and Northampton Town — but Feethams remained as one of the few locations where these two sports survived in such proximity until the recent move. The cricket pavilion dates from 1906; unfortunately the twin-tower gateway is not shown. Of the football ground in the early 1960s, three sides had received some covered accommodation. The East Stand was built between 1914 and 1919, shortly before Darlington became founder members of the Third Division (North) in 1921. This was followed in the mid-1920s by the construction of a short West Stand; the structure seen here was opened in August 1961 following fire damage to the original structure in September 1960 (ironically on the same night that the Quakers played their first floodlit match at the ground). Finally in 1960, a cover was built over the Cricket Field (North) End. Both the Cricket Field End cover and the short West Stand still survive; the old East Stand, however, has disappeared and a new stand constructed in its place in 1998. Following a period of uncertainty — and a season (1989/90) based in the Vauxhall Conference — the club at that stage decided against relocation in favour of modernising Feethams; the new East Stand was part of a programme that was planned to see the ground upgraded. The future of Feethams was again brought into doubt when local businessman George Reynolds took over the club in 1999. He announced ambitious plans for the construction of a new stadium at Neasham Road with the intention that the new

ground would be ready for the start of the 2001/02 season; in the event, problems with financing the new stadium resulted in league football continuing at Feethams until the end of the 2002/03 season. The new Reynolds Arena, with its 25,000 capacity opened at the start of the 2003/04 campaign. However, Darlington collapsed into Administration during the course of the season and, for a period, it appeared that the team would return to Feethams. However, with the Sterling Consortium taking over, the club will remain at the new stadium, albeit a stadium now devoid of its original 'Reynolds Arena' sobriquet.

Right: 1964 (A127992)
Below: 2003 (695511)

Derby County

Then: 20 September 1952
Now: 15 June 2004

Founded in 1884, Derby County moved to the Baseball Ground in 1895; the first game in its permanent occupation occurred on 14 September 1895, although an earlier game (in 1892) had also been played there and the ground had been used for a number of sports, including baseball, from the 1880s. The 1952 view shows the Baseball Ground as it existed prior to the construction of the second tier on the Popular Side (in 1969) and those changes which converted the ground into an all-seater stadium for the last period of its life as a Premiership stadium. Closest to the camera is the Main Stand; this was the result of a rebuild that opened in September 1926 which became known as the ABC Stand. Opposite, the Popular Side was covered in the late 1920s. This work was followed by the covering of both Normanton and Ormaston ends with the result that the Baseball Ground provided covered accommodation in part or in whole on all four sides of the ground by 1933.

The future of the Baseball Ground was uncertain for a number of years, but initially the club decided to face the post-Taylor environment by upgrading the existing ground. However, in a complete volte-face, it was announced on 21 February 1996 that the club would relocate to a new ground — to be named eventually Pride Park — situated to the east of the city centre. Work on this new ground enabled it to be opened for the 1997/98 season. The new ground initially had an all-seater capacity of just over 30,000. The final stage in the Pride Park redevelopment occurred in 1999 with the construction of the corner stand between the South and West stands, which takes the ground's capacity to 33,597, all seated. Initially, the Baseball Ground was retained for reserve and youth team matches; the former, however, transferred to Pride Park and the ground has subsequently been demolished.

Below: 2004 (697487)
Right: 1952 (R17766)

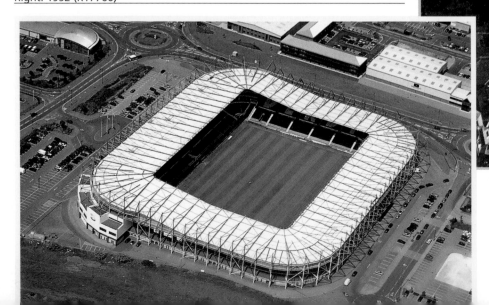

Doncaster Rovers

Then: 1953
Now: 15 May 2003

Belle Vue has been the home of Doncaster Rovers for more than 80 years, with the club having moved there originally in 1922, the year before the team was elected to the Third Division (North). The ground, located close to the town's racecourse and early airport, had its original foundations and banks constructed from ash. The early facilities included a stand on the north side, which was later lengthened, and a 700-seat stand at the west end. This latter structure had been transferred from the previous ground at Bennetthorpe. The south, Popular, side was covered in 1938. As a result of safety concerns following the Bradford City fire in 1985 the ex-Bennetthorpe stand was condemned and, two years later, in 1987, the Popular Side cover was removed as a result of the bank upon which it was constructed subsiding. The top half of the side was fenced off and, in 1989, a new cantilevered roof was raised over the remaining section of the side. In the decade after 1985 some £0.75m was spent on safety measures at the ground. The floodlights were originally installed in March 1952 and a third installation inaugurated in 1992. The Main Stand was seriously damaged by fire, under suspicious circumstances, in 1995, causing some £200,000 of damage. In 1998, Rovers dropped out of the Football League, only reclaiming their league status at the end of the 2002/03 season. The club has plans, now that its League status has been restored, to relocate to a new 10,000-seat stadium to be shared with the town's Rugby League team and Doncaster Belles Ladies FC. It is hoped that the new £20 million stadium will be available from the start of the 2005/06 season.

Far right: 1953 (A49621)
Right: 2003 (695661)

Everton

Then: 12 May 1950
Now: 15 May 2003

Goodison Park has been the home of Everton for more than a century but, in 1997, following a referendum amongst fans, which voted in favour of a move, the club announced that it planned to relocate. However, as related later, these plans are now in doubt.

Although Everton played its first game at Goodison on 1 September 1892 — the ground had actually opened for an athletics meeting the previous month — the club itself had been founded in 1878 (as St Domingo's FC becoming Everton the following year) and became a founder member of the Football League in 1888; between 1884 and 1892, when the club fell out with the ground's owner, Everton played at Anfield. The first of these two views, taken in 1950, shows the ground as it was completely developed to the designs of Archibald Leitch. Although not physically part of the ground, the church of St Lukes, built in 1901, has affected the development of the ground. On all four sides of the ground are two-tiered stands designed by Leitch and built over a 30-year period. The first phase of Leitch's work was the Park End Stand; this was completed in 1907. This was followed two years later by the Main Stand. In 1926 the Bullens Road Stand was constructed followed in 1938 by the Gladwys Road End; the Bullen Road and Gladwys Street stands were linked at the same time.

Whilst the ground appears today to be radically different, this is only true in part as both the Bullens Road and Gladwys Street stands have only been reroofed and fitted with seats. The major new works are the Main Stand, with its three tiers, which was completed in 1969-70 and the new Park End Stand, which was opened in August 1994. The ground's capacity is currently an all-seater 40,200 but, if the plans to relocate proceed, then the club will be moving to a new stadium with a planned seating capacity of up to 60,000. Over the past few years, however, the proposed move has been the subject of much debate as control of the club has changed. The position when the second edition of this book was completed was that relocation was progressing. A second poll of fans in early 2001 indicated a continuing high level of support for the project and the club investigated the possibilities of constructing a new 55,000-seat capacity ground in the King's Dock area of the city. However, these plans were abandoned in the spring of 2003 when the cost of the development proved to be excessive. However, the club is still keen to relocate and is currently investigating a scheme to move to a new 55,000-seat stadium at Central Docks. There is, however, no definite timescale for any move at present.

Far left: 1950 (R12325)

Left: 2003 (695677)

Fulham

Then: 12 May 1958
Now: 15 June 2004

In the recent history of football, few clubs have had a more controversial existence than Fulham, whose ground has been the subject of much dispute. Today, with the club in the ownership of another colourful chairman, in the form of Harrods' owner Mohamed Al-Fayed, the future looks more secure as money has been spent on both squad and ground; however, like many chairmen before him, Al-Fayed has discovered that massive expenditure on players and manager did not guarantee immediate success. Fulham FC was established as St Andrews in 1879; after moving to Craven Cottage in 1894, the club played its first game at the ground on 10 October 1896. The club joined the Football League in 1907. The rudimentary facilities offered at Craven Cottage in 1958 are all too evident in the 'Then' shot. As illustrated, Craven Cottage was still very much the product of Archibald Leitch's involvement in the first decade of the 20th century. In 1905, before the club joined the League, Leitch designed the famous corner pavilion, as well as the Stevenage Road Stand and the three open sides. These open sides as illustrated here — the Riverside Terrace alongside the Thames, the Hammersmith and Putney ends — were destined to remain unchanged until the early 1960s.

As can be seen in the 'Now' photograph, Craven Cottage now provides cover on four sides. The Riverside Terrace was roofed in April 1972 — as the Eric Miller Stand (named after one erstwhile chairman) — and has subsequently been fitted, in 1997, with seats. The corner pavilion and Stevenage Road Stand were both listed in March 1987 and, as can be seen, work was undertaken on the latter in the late 1990s. The Hammersmith End was extended in 1961 and covered at the rear four years later. Floodlighting was installed in 1962. In 1998 revolution came to Craven Cottage when Harrods boss Mohamed Al-Fayed took over. With his backing the club moved from the Second to the First Division at the end of the 1998/99 season and, two years later, up to the Premiership, bringing back terraces for one season to English football's top flight. However, the club's rapid rise brought with it the need to redevelop its ground and the club had ambitious plans for the reconstruction of the ground with planning permission being granted towards the end of the 2000/01 season for the construction of a 30,000 all-seater stadium costing £55 million on the existing site. All of the existing ground — including the famous cottage — was to have been swept away with the exception of the facade along Stevenage Road. It was anticipated that work would commence at the end of the 2001/02 season with Fulham ground sharing during the 2002/03 season, prior to occupying its new facility in August 2003. However, the redevelopment did not proceed as planned and, after two years at Loftus Road, Fulham returned to an upgraded Craven Cottage in August 2004. The work at Craven Cottage included the installation of seats on the remaining terraces and the provision of a roof over the uncovered Putney End and an extended roof over the Hammersmith End. As completed, the stadium can now provide seating for some 22,000 fans.

Left: 1958 (A70736)
Above: 2004 (697369)

Gillingham

Then: 14 July 1972
Now: 17 May 2004

Apart from Maidstone, whose presence in the Football League was both short-lived and not particularly successful, the county of Kent has not been well represented in the professional game. The club that has kept the flag flying in this corner of England is Gillingham, for most of its career the only League team from the county. The name Gillingham was adopted in 1913; for the first 20 years of the club's life at Priestfield — where the club played its first game on 2 September 1893 — the team was known as New Brompton. The club joined the Football League in 1920 and survived until 1938, when it was replaced by Ipswich Town. League status was regained in 1950. The 'Then' shot shows the ground as it was in the early 1970s. Of particular note are the Gordon Road Stand, which was built in 1899 and which was (until its closure in 1985) the oldest surviving stand in the English game, the Main Stand, which dated from 1914 but which had been refurbished and reroofed in 1965, and the covered Rainham End (work which was completed in 1927 as part of a programme undertaken once the club joined the League). Floodlighting was installed in 1963-4. Today, there have been major changes, including the rebuilt Gordon Road Stand; the original was condemned as a result of the Bradford fire and demolished in 1989. The new structure was completed in 1996. Earlier work, in 1975, included the installation of seats in the Main Stand paddock. As elsewhere, the fortunes of the club declined in the late 1980s/early 1990s, and it was in 1995 that the team was rescued by Paul Scally. Under his control, there has been considerable work at Priestfield, including the aforementioned Gordon Road Stand, raising the ground's capacity to about 11,000. After a period when the club seriously examined the possibility of relocation, this was abandoned in favour of upgrading of the existing

facilities at Priestfield at least in the short term.

Work commenced on the construction of the new two-tier Main (Medway) and Rainham End stands in 1999; the latter was completed by the start of the 2000/01 season, whilst work on the former was completed during the course of the season. The open Gillingham Town End was demolished during late 2003 and replaced by a temporary stand as shown in the 'Now' photograph. It is intended that this be replaced by a new 3,200-seat covered stand to be named after Brian Moore. Despite the investment in Priestfield, there remains the possibility that the club will relocate although there is no timescale for such as move at present.

Right: 1972 (A238673)
Below: 2004 (697300)

Grimsby Town

Then: 10 June 1968
Now: 1996

Grimsby Town was founded in 1878 and in 1892 became one of the founder members of the Second Division of the Football League. Forced out from the most recent of their previous grounds — Abbey Park — Town played their first game at Blundell Park (which, ironically is situated in neighbouring Cleethorpes) on 2 September 1899. Part of the ground — the Cleethorpes End and along the Grimsby Road side — utilised structures transferred from Abbey Park; these had already been replaced by the date of the 'Then' photograph.

The ground as illustrated in 1968 shows well its proximity to the North Sea. The Main Stand was built in 1901 and was extended to the southeast corner of the ground between 1929 and 1932. Opposite the Main Stand is the 60yd-long Barrett Stand; this was constructed in 1926 to replace one of the two structures transferred from the old Abbey Park ground. The stand was flanked on both sides by wooden terracing. The second ex-Abbey Park structure, located at the South (Cleethorpes) End, was replaced by the Osmond Stand in 1939; at the same time this was linked to the existing Main Stand to create the 'L'-shaped structure visible. The Pontoon Stand, at the North (Grimsby) End of the ground, was completed in 1961. Floodlighting was first installed in 1953 but was modified in 1960 to the condition illustrated here.

As can be seen, the more recent view illustrates how little Blundell Park has changed over the years. The Main Stand, the Osmond Stand and the Pontoon Stand are still extant, although the 1926-built Barrett Stand was demolished in 1980 and replaced by the new Findus (later Stones Bitter) Stand, which opened in 1982. At the same time seating was installed in the Main Stand paddock. The ground is now all-seater, with a capacity of some 11,000, with the result that the wooden terraces alongside the Findus Stand are no more. Town received a year's extension for the seating work to be completed, with work commencing in May 1995.

However, time would appear to be running out for Blundell Park as the club had ambitious plans for the construction of a new 20,000-seat ground at Great Coates. However, as with a number of schemes elsewhere, the original time-scale proved optimistic. The revised plan involved a reduced, 14,000-seat, stadium at Great Coates costing some £14 million and to be sponsored by Conoco. However, there is no definite time-scale at present. But this has also been thrown into doubt as a result of the club's failure to acquire the site; it is possible that relocation will still be progressed, however, but at an alternative location.

Above: 1968 (A186713)
Right: 1996 (655124)

Hartlepool United

Then: 10 August 1972
Now: 9 May 2003

The history of the Victoria Ground at Hartlepool stretches back to the late 19th century. It was originally opened on 27 October 1886 for use by the local Rugby team. It was some 20 years later that the newly-formed Hartlepools United played its first game at the ground on 2 September 1908. The original site was split in half at this time with the southern section being used for the greyhound racing circuit. United joined the Football League in 1921 and, apart from a brief period of success under Brian Clough, has spent most of its career battling for survival both financially and in ensuring league football. The earlier of these two photographs shows the ground in the early 1970s. At this stage the Victoria Ground comprised a stand parallel to Clarence Road — of which more anon — two covered terraces (the Ice Rink End — although by this date the ice rink had been demolished — and the Town End), and the new (1968-built) cantilevered Mill House Stand. This view shows clearly the relationship between the football ground and the greyhound stadium. The Main Stand had been erected as a temporary structure in 1919 following the demolition of the earlier stand as a result of a Zeppelin bombing raid on 27 November 1916. In the event, the temporary stand was to survive until after the Bradford fire of May 1985, it was demolished. This demolition was followed by the removal of the roofs over the covered terraces at the Ice Rink and Town ends in March 1986. At this time the ground's capacity was reduced to 3,300. Today, as can be seen from the more recent photograph, the Victoria Ground is once again covered on all four sides. In 1990 the Ice Rink End was again reroofed and, two years later, seats were installed. In July 1995 a new, 1,650-seat stand was constructed along Clarence Road; this was named after the late Cyril Knowles, who was once manager of United. In the same year the Town End was modernised and a new roof installed. Combined with the still extant Mill House Stand, this means that today the Victoria Ground has a capacity of 7,629. There are plans for the further development of the ground, including the incorporation of a leisure centre, starting with the reconstruction of the Mill House stand, but there is no definite time-scale at present. Note that the greyhound track has been demolished; this work was undertaken early in 1998.

Left: 1972 (A240119)

Below: 2003 (695498)

Huddersfield Town

Then: 25 July 1949
Now: 15 May 2003

Huddersfield Town was formed in September 1908 and played its first game at Leeds Road on the second of that month. Ambitious from the start, the club applied to join the League and was admitted at the start of the 1911/12 season. By this stage, the club had already had Archibald Leitch design a ground fit for the league at Leeds Road; the facilities opened officially on 2 September 1911. The 'Then' shot shows Leeds Road as it existed in 1949, immediately prior to the fire of 3 April 1950 which destroyed the roof and upper tier of the Main Stand. The ground as illustrated here was very much the work of Leitch; his plans envisaged the rotation of the original pitch by 90°, the construction of a Main Stand (with his trademark gable end in the middle — clearly visible in this shot), a covered Leeds Road End (although the structure illustrated here dates from 1929; it was popularly known as the 'Cowshed') and open terraces. Between the Main Stand and the Cowshed was an L-shaped stand; this structure had been bought second-hand from Fleetwood and was used as a schoolboys' stand. In the 1930s and 1940s the open terracing was improved — evidence of this work is clearly evident by the terracing opposite the Main Stand — which was sufficiently good to withstand inspection in the 1970s and 1980s. Subsequent to this photograph, the Main Stand was rebuilt after the fire and the Popular Side was covered in 1955. The second photograph shows the new Alfred McAlpine stadium. Town had been considering relocation from the mid-1980s and on 12 August 1992 planning permission was given to the construction of the new ground. Leeds Road saw its last League game on 30 April 1994 with the first game at the new stadium occurring on 20 August 1994. At this time only the Riverside and Kilner Bank stands were complete; the third (South) stand was opened in December 1994. Work started on the construction of the final (North) stand in 1997 with the intention of having it ready for the 1998/99 season, which aim was achieved. Completion of the North Stand took the capacity of the McAlpine Stadium to 24,500.

Right: 1949 (A25260)
Inset: 2003 (695672)

Hull City

Then: 17 July 1972
Now: 9 May 2003

Boothferry Park was one of the more recent of the first generation of football grounds to be covered in this book, seeing its first game played on 31 August 1946. The history of Hull City, however, stretches back to the club's formation in 1904. The team was elected to the Football League in 1905 but played at a number of grounds before acquiring the site of Boothferry Park in 1930. A combination, however, of lack of funds and World War 2 meant that the ground could not be occupied until after the war. When the new ground opened, it consisted of the West Stand (built in 1946), terraces (dating from the prewar work) and a small cover over the North End. The view in 1972 shows the ground at its peak. The terraces had been extended in 1949, the North Stand enlarged in 1950 and, on 6 January 1951, trains first used the Boothferry Park Halt on the adjacent railway line. Also in 1951 the East Side terrace was covered. Floodlighting had been first installed in 1953, but the

equipment illustrated here dated from replacement work in October 1964. An indoor sports hall was built behind the South End in 1963 and, two years later, a new South Stand was constructed. Latterly much of Boothferry Park was unchanged. The South Stand, West Stand and the East Side terrace remained; the only main difference came at the North End, where the covered accommodation was demolished in 1982, shortly after the club went into receivership, to be replaced with a supermarket and a new small terrace. Since 1982, the future of Boothferry Park had been uncertain; in the summer of 1997, for example, it was announced that Hull City would share grounds with Hull Sharks RLFC and vacate Boothferry Park. This proposal collapsed when Hull City was in fact taken over by ex-tennis player David Lloyd. Under Lloyd's stewardship, plans were developed for the redevelopment of the existing ground; however, these were to come to nothing and, between the first two editions of this book, City was faced by several crises, including being locked out of the ground both before and during the 2000/01 season.

By this date, however, Hull City's future was away from Boothferry Park, as the City Council, flush with money from the partial sale of its local telephone company, decided to fund the construction of a new £44 million stadium to be shared by City and Hull Sharks RLFC. The new Kingston Communications Stadium, with its 25,404 capacity, opened on 19 December 2002. The West Stand is provided with two tiers and there are plans to construct a second tier on the East Stand, taking capacity to 30,000, if required.

Left: 1972 (A234734)
Right: 2003 (695555)

Ipswich Town

Then: 17 October 1970
Now: 18 February 2003

Although Ipswich Town was formed in 1878 it was not until 1936 that the club turned professional and entered the Southern League. Champions in the club's first season, Town were elected to the Football League in 1938, replacing Gillingham and from that point would start the team's steady rise to the old First Division championship, FA Cup success and European football. There have been few more dramatic stories in the history of English football. The 'Then' photograph shows the 'old' Portman Road as it existed before the developments of the 1970s onwards. On the right hand side of the photograph is the old East Stand; this had been constructed and extended in the late 1930s when the club turned professional. Opposite is the West Stand; this was built in 1957 and extended to the full length of the pitch in 1958. The North and Churchmans ends were covered in the late 1930s. The redevelopment of Portman Road, as illustrated in the more recent photograph, started soon after the 'Then' photograph was taken. The East Stand was replaced by the Portman Stand; this opened in August 1971. It was to be further modified with the addition of seating in the paddock and the construction of executive boxes in 1978. In February 1984 a new tier was opened on top of the existing West Stand; this work cost £1.4 million and saw the stand rechristened as the 'Pioneer Stand'. Again this was modified in 1990 by the addition of seating in the former paddock. Finally, in 1992, seating was installed at both the North and Churchmans ends; at the same time the existing covers

at both ends were extended over the new seats. This meant that Portman Road became the first all-seater stadium in the Premiership, some two years before it was mandatory. This resulted in the ground having a capacity of some 22,600, which was small by Premiership standards (Ipswich having regained its Premiership position at the end of the 1999/00 season after several years in the First). Work started during the course of the 2000/01 season on the reconstruction of the Churchman's (South) Stand and the work was virtually complete by the end of the season. Planning permission was also granted for the reconstruction of the North Stand; despite local opposition, construction of the new 7,035-seat stand went ahead, with work being completed in 2003. The total capacity at Portman Road is now 30,226.

Left: 1970 (A207758)
Below: 2003 (694284)

Kidderminster Harriers

Then: 28 October 1971
Now: 9 February 2004

Founded primarily as an athletics team in 1877 before turning to football in 1886, Kidderminster Harriers moved to Aggborough Stadium in May 1890, a ground which had had rugby played on it for some years. The club, however, folded in 1901 but was reconstituted and gradually progressed through the non-league structure. Harriers finally achieved Nationwide League status at the end of the 1999/00 season, having been cruelly denied promotion six years earlier when it was deemed that the club's wooden stand was not up to League standards. Protestations by the club at the time that the stand was scheduled for replacement fell on deaf ears.

The first of these photographs illustrates the ground as it existed at the start of the 1970s. The oval shape of the ground — a consequence of the club's background in athletics — is all too readily apparent in the view. The Main Stand, with its 460-seat capacity is on the west side of the ground. This structure was opened on 31 August 1935. The original roof of the stand originally covered only the seating area; it was subsequently extended — as shown here — to cover the paddock. It was this structure that contributed significantly to the failure of Harriers to gain admission to the League in May 1994. Opposite the Main Stand is the Cow Shed; this was erected in the 1920s as a replacement for an earlier stand. The floodlighting illustrated dated from 1966 and was a replacement for an earlier installation dating from the early 1950s.

Today, the ground is radically different and evidence of the club's origins as an athletics club has largely disappeared. The Cow Shed, which was partially demolished by a gale in 1975 (but subsequently repaired), was initially replaced by the Bill Greaves Stand in 1979. Terracing behind the two goals was installed in the early 1980s, when the oval shape of the ground was largely eradicated. The terraces were covered in the 1990s. The Main Stand was rebuilt in 1994. By this time, the ground's current capacity was just over 6,200, of which just over 1,100 were seated. The next phase of the development of the ground was the replacement of the Bill Greaves Stand, which was demolished in February 2003; a new £1.5 million structure, providing 2,040 seats, was completed later the same year, taking the ground's capacity to 6,229 (of which 3,177 are seated).

Right: 1971 (A220762)
Below: 2004 (696961)

Leeds United

Then: 16 March 1967
Now: 15 June 2004

Although Leeds United itself only dates back to the immediate post World War 1 era — the club was admitted to the Football League in 1920 — football in the city and the Elland Road ground itself both have long pedigrees. The original League club in the city, Leeds City, was established in 1904 and played its first game (at Elland Road) on 15 October of that year; the club had been formed from members of an earlier club (Hunslet) and joined the Football League in 1905. The orientation of the present ground owes much to the presence of Leeds City; however, the club was to be expelled from the Football League in 1919 for making illegal payments to players. Elland Road itself dates from the late 1870s and was used initially for rugby. After the failure of the rugby club in 1883, the ground was used as a sports ground by a local brewery. At this time the ground was known the Old Peacock, after the adjacent Peacock Pub (from which, incidentally, the present Leeds United derives its nickname). In 1897, Holbeck, one of the early members of the Northern Rugby Union — as the Rugby League was then known — moved to the ground. Unfortunately, its tenure was destined to be brief and it ceased playing in 1904, thus opening the way for Leeds City.

The first of these two photographs shows the ground as it existed in 1967 when the Don Revie era was about to bring the club a period of sustained success. The March date is significant because it was during this month that a barrier collapsed on the Lowfields Road side; fortunately, there were no fatalities but the urgent need for modernisation was all too apparent. The Main (West) Stand was constructed in the mid-1950s after a fire on 18 September 1956 destroyed the original; the new stand was opened on 31 August 1957. Opposite the Main Stand is the Lowfields Road Stand; this was constructed over the existing terrace in three stages from the late 1920s, being completed in 1933. The covered South (Elland Road) End was provided with a wooden roof a decade earlier; this replaced an earlier structure. The Kop at the north end of the ground was extended at the same period, with the terracing being extended to cover also the northeast corner.

The more recent photographs shows the developments of the past 30 years well. In the foreground, the West (Main) Stand built in 1956/57 remains, although it has been extended to link into the northwest corner (constructed in 1970). In front of the stand is the £1.3 million banqueting suite that was constructed in 1991. The northeast corner was covered in 1971. Three

years later, in 1974, the pitch was moved slightly to the north; this allowed for construction of the 7,500-capacity (including 3,500 seats) South Stand at a cost of £0.5 million. The southeast corner was covered in 1991 at a cost of £0.82 million; this provided an additional 1,300 seats. In 1992 the Lowfields Road Stand was replaced by the new East Stand; this structure, which has the largest cantilevered roof in Europe, cost £6.5 million and provides all-seater accommodation for 17,000. Finally, in 1994, the old covered Kop, which had received a roof in 1968, was refurbished at a price of £1.2 million to provide 6,800 seats; now known as the Don Revie Stand, the structure was officially opened on 16 October 1994. Today, Elland Road's all-seater capacity is 40,000.

In contemporary football, however, a capacity of 40,000 is deemed insufficient for a team of Leeds's ambition and towards the end of the 2000/01 season it was announced that the club intended either to relocate or to expand Elland Road, with the intention of achieving a capacity of 50,000. However, there was no timescale announced and, following the club's failure to build on its European success at the end of that season resulting in its now well-known financial problems — allied to relegation at the end of 2003/04 from the Premiership — it's uncertain if and when any redevelopment or relocation will take place.

Right: 1967 (A169317)
Below: 2004 (697477)

Leicester City

Then: 11 June 1969
Now: 6 May 2003

Founded as Leicester Fosse in 1884, the future Leicester City — the club was renamed in 1919 — moved into Filbert Street in 1891, playing their first game in November of that year. Leicester Fosse entered the Football League in 1894. In the pre-World War 1 era, the development of the ground was much influenced by Archibald Leitch, but the ground that is featured in the first of these two photographs was largely the result of developments post-1920. On 26 November 1921 a new Main Stand was opened. This was, however, partially destroyed during World War 2 and the Main Stand illustrated here was largely the result of rebuilding work in 1949. The next development was the construction of a double-deck stand over the Spion Kop in 1927; this — the South Stand — opened on 26 November 1927. This was followed in the 1930s by the covering of the Popular Side. Floodlights were installed in 1957. Latterly, Filbert Street was largely the same on three sides, although there were detailed differences which will be discussed later. The major difference was the construction of the new Main Stand; this £6 million structure, which provided the ground with 9,500 seats, was completed in December 1993 and gave the ground a lop-sided look. Elsewhere, seats were first fitted into the Filbert Street Terrace — which became the North Stand — in 1971 and four years later the roof was raised slightly to accommodate executive boxes. Seats were fitted into the South Stand in 1994 when the ground was converted into an all-seater form. Filbert Street finally had a capacity of just under 23,000, which made it one of the smaller grounds in the Premiership. In mid-1998 Leicester City announced that, like neighbouring Derby County, the club was to relocate to a new 40,000 all-seater stadium. However,

the scheme was much delayed and the initial date for the opening of the new stadium — August 2000 — proved wildly optimistic. Having identified a site, belonging to Powergen at Freemans Wharf (slightly to the south of Filbert Street), work on the new Walkers Stadium, as the ground was named, progressed to allow the team to move in at the start of the 2002/03 season. The new stadium, which cost £28 million and provides seats for 32,500, is designed to allow for the construction of a second tier on the East Stand, if required, to take the capacity to 40,000. Following the move, Filbert Street has been demolished for redevelopment.

Below: 1969 (A194726)
Right: 2003 (695613)

Leyton Orient

Then: 28 June 1960
Now: 14 June 2004

For the first 50 years of its life, Leyton Orient (as it became after World War 2 and again after 1987) occupied a number of grounds — including the Millfields Road ground that later became the Clapton Greyhound Stadium — before settling at Brisbane Road in 1937. Founded as Clapton Orient in 1888, the club replaced the Leyton Amateurs at Brisbane Road, playing its first game there on 28 August 1937. The Amateurs had played at Brisbane Road since 1905. Orient inherited a ground with a stand on one side — the west — and with terraces on the remaining three sides. The 'Then' shot, taken shortly before Orient's one and only season in the First Division, shows both the old West Stand and the new East (Main) Stand, which had been built in 1956 and which was damaged by fire on completion. Floodlights had been inaugurated earlier in 1960. One major difference is the disappearance of the South Terrace and its replacement by a new small South Stand. The old terrace was demolished in 1996 and the site stood empty for a couple of seasons. The original plans envisaged the construction of a 3,000-seat stand on the site, but in the event these proposals had to be scaled down and a 1,300-seat structure — illustrated here — was completed for the 1999/2000. The club — which was acquired by Barry Hearn in March 1995 — has plans for the further redevelopment of the ground and received a £1 million grant from the Football Trust for the construction of a new West Stand in December 2000. The next phase in the ground's redevelopment, which started after the end of the 2003/04 season, with the demolition of the East Stand and North Terrace, is for rebuilding on the north and westsides. The work will include the construction of residential blocks at each corner of the ground and the construction of new North and West stands. Once the work is completed, the ground will have an all-seated capacity of 11,000 although with demolition of the West Stand and North Terrace, capacity for 2004/05 will be much reduced.

Left: 1960 (A81492)
Below: 2004 (697464)

Lincoln City

Then: 30 June 1972
Now: 18 May 2004

Lincoln City were founded in October 1884 and became founder members of the new Second Division of the Football League in 1892. Three years later, on 2 September 1895, the Imps played their first game at Sincil Bank. The ground as illustrated in the 'Then' photograph sees the ground prior to the collapse of the South Park Terrace perimeter in September 1975. The Main Stand on the east of the ground was constructed in 1932. The previous year, 1931, had seen the Railway (North) End terrace concreted and partially covered; this cover was extended over the east corner of the ground in 1957. The Sincil Bank Terrace, on the west of the ground, had been covered until 1948. Floodlighting was installed in 1962.

The ground today is dramatically different. Not only was Lincoln City the unfortunate team to be playing Bradford City at Valley Parade when the fire occurred, but the team also suffered further trauma when an aircraft bringing the players back after an overseas trip overshot the runway at Leeds-Bradford Airport. Sincil Bank was also a casualty in the aftermath of the fire: much of the ground was condemned. The Railway End was dismantled in 1985 and the Stacey West Stand — named after the two Lincoln City victims of the Bradford fire — was opened in August 1990. In 1986 the old Main Stand was demolished, to be replaced by a new Main Stand in November 1987. By that time, City had suffered another disaster — automatic relegation to the Conference at the end of the 1986/87 season. Fortunately automatic promotion

was gained at the first attempt. The opening of the new Main Stand was followed in August 1992 by the opening of the new South Park Stand. A small Family Stand was constructed next to the Main Stand; this opened in March 1994. Finally, in March 1995 the 6,189-seat Linpave Stand was opened; this was named after the firm which both built and sponsored the stand. The Stacey West Stand was for a couple of seasons in the mid-1990s made part terrace, with seating removed from both wing, but this was reversed and Sincil Bank is now all-seater, with a current capacity of just under 11,000.

Below: 2004 (697257)
Right: 1972 (A235406)

Liverpool

Then: 28 May 1966
Now: 15 May 2003

As already noted under the entry for Everton, Anfield was used for League football well before Liverpool FC was formed in 1892 and played first at Anfield on 1 September of that year. The ground itself saw Everton first play on 28 September 1884. The first of these two photographs shows the stadium as it existed in the mid-1960s just when the team was beginning to become one of the dominant forces in English (and European) football. The main stand, with the characteristic gable that marked many of Archibald Leitch's designs, dated from 1906 when Leitch undertook a considerable upgrading of the existing facilities. The enormous Kop was covered in 1928. Opposite the Main Stand was the Kemlyn Road Stand; the structure illustrated here had been opened on 22 August 1964 replacing an earlier structure. The fourth side of the ground, the Anfield Road End, had had its roof replaced in 1964. Apart from the actual ground, note in the corner by the Kop (next to Kemlyn Road) the club flagpole; this came from the Brunel-designed *Great Eastern* which had ended its days on the Mersey.

Although Anfield is a fairly confined site, the club has undertaken considerable work to upgrade the facilities. This included the purchase of houses along Kemlyn Road to enable a new stand to be built; this work, involving the construction of a second tier, was completed for opening on 1 September 1992. Inevitably, this led the new structure to become known as the Centenary Stand. Opposite the Main Stand had been extended in the early 1970s, opening officially on 10 March 1973; seats were installed in the paddock in 1980. The Kop bade an emotional farewell to the last standing fans in April 1994 and the new Kop Stand was completed for the following season. The final stage of the redevelopment of Anfield came with the approval in October 1995 for the reconstruction of the Anfield Road Stand. This work was completed in 1997 and takes Anfield's all-seater capacity to 45,000.

The future for Anfield is, however, not bright as the club wishes to increase capacity — essential if it is to remain competitive with teams like Manchester United and the major European clubs — and, having examined the possibility of further expansion at Anfield, has decided to relocate. Having examined the options, the club announced in May 2003 that it intended to construct a new 60,000-seat ground at Stanley Park costing some £80 million to be available from the start of the 2006/07 season. The local council gave the go-ahead to the scheme in late July 2004.

Right: 1966 (A162056)
Inset: 2003 (695690)

Luton Town

Then: 25 May 1954
Now: 6 May 2003

Kenilworth Road has, in recent years, been one of the most controversial grounds in English football; it was one of the pioneers of artificial pitches and was also to operate a ban on away fans for a number of years. The confined location of the ground is all too evident in these two photographs. Bounded on one side by the Luton-Dunstable railway line and later by a realigned railway alongside the 1987-built link road and by houses elsewhere, the ground is ill-suited for major development. For more than a decade Town have been investigating the possibilities of relocation, but these plans have yet to come to fruition, with the result that today the ground has a capacity of 9,975 all-seated. The football club was formed in 1885 and moved to Kenilworth Road 20 years later, playing its first game there on 4 September 1905. The first of the two photographs shows the ground in 1954. The Main Stand dates from the early 1920s when it was rebuilt using a structure obtained from Kempton Park Racecourse after the original stand had burnt down. The Kenilworth Road End was still open terrace; this was extended in the late 1930s. The Ivy Road Terrace was covered in 1933; known as the Bobbers Stand, this area was to be converted into executive boxes in 1985. In 1935 the Oak Road Terrace was covered and in 1937 this cover was extended to meet the Main Stand. The more recent photograph shows clearly the survival of the Main Stand. In the foreground, the Park Road Terrace was extended at the rear in 1955; this view also shows how the terrace is accessed through the ground floor of houses along Oak Road. After the installation of executive boxes in the Ivy Road Terrace, seats were fitted in the Oak Road End and the Kenilworth Road End was covered; it was this work which led to the club's controversial ban on away fans. The New Stand, linking the Main Stand with the Kenilworth Road End, was completed in 1991.

For a number of years prior to 1998 the club was controlled by Simon Kohler, who had ambitious plans for the construction of a new ground — the Kohlerdome — but, during the 1998/99 season, the club went into Administration and this threw all future plans into abeyance. However, the club was rescued by a consortium led by Mike Watson-Challis during 2000 and plans for relocation resurfaced as a result. During February 2001 the club acquired a 55-acre site close to Junction 10 of the M1, although any proposed redevelopment still required planning consent. One of a number of clubs to enter Administration following the collapse of ITV Digital, in the summer of 2004 it was announced that the new consortium hoping to take-over the club still intended to relocate, but there is still no definite timescale.

Below: 1954 (A54388)
Right: 2003 (695591)

Macclesfield Town

Then: 26 July 1955
Now: 18 May 2004

Although Macclesfield Town were only admitted to the Football League at the start of the 1997/98 season (in place of Hereford United), having been rejected at the end of 1994/95 when the team finished top of the Vauxhall Conference due to the condition of the ground, this was not the first time that Town's Moss Rose ground had played host to Football League action. During the period between 1990 and 1992 Chester City played their home games in neighbouring Macclesfield whilst the new Deva Stadium was being completed. Macclesfield Town itself was founded as a rugby club in 1874 and played for the first 17 years of its life at Rostron Field before moving to Moss Rose in 1891. The original Macclesfield club went bankrupt in 1897 and was replaced at Moss Rose by a new club, Hallfield FC, which was rechristened Macclesfield Town in 1904.

The first of these two photographs shows the ground as it existed in the mid-1950s. The area behind each goal mouth has not, as yet, been formally terraced, although there is covered accommodation on both sides. The original wooden stand, dating from 1906, is on the north side. This original stand was replaced in 1968 by the cantilevered structure visible in the more recent photograph. Floodlighting was first introduced at Moss Rose at the start of the 1965/66 season. Other changes over the past 40 years have included the installation of terracing behind both goal mouths; this work was undertaken in the late 1980s. The cover was added to the Star Lane (South) Stand prior to the club's admission to the Football League, at which time seating was also installed on the former terracing in order to meet League requirements.

Since entering the Nationwide League, Macclesfield achieved promotion to the Second Division, but failed to sustain that level and were immediately relegated back to the Third. However, the period has seen further work take place at Moss Rose with the opening of the new £1.45 million 1,497-seat Estate Road (Alfred McAlpine) Stand, which opened officially on 5 May 2001. The next phase of the ground's redevelopment will see a second tier — with seating — over the existing terrace at the Silkman End.

Below: 1955 (R25050)
Right: 2004 (697243)

Manchester City

Then: 1923
Now: 18 May 2004

It was only in 1923 that Manchester City moved to its ground at Maine Road, playing the club's first game there on 25 August of that year. The first of these two photographs shows the facilities on offer at that time. The club's origins date back to 1880 when a team called West Gorton was formed; as Ardwick this team entered the Football League in 1892 but collapsed two years later to be replaced by Manchester City. Prior to moving to Maine Road, City played at Hyde Road. As can be seen, in 1923 Maine Road was somewhat Spartan, with three sides of open banking and with the Main Stand providing the only covered accommodation.

Fortunately, for City fans, despite the problems in the boardroom and on the pitch (which saw the team relegated to the Second Division at the end of the 1997/98 season), facilities at Maine Road improved dramatically. The North Stand, which replaced the open Scoreboard End, was completed in 1971. The Main Stand was reroofed in 1982. In 1992 the old Platt Lane Stand (which had been covered in 1938 and lined by a curved roof to the Main Stand in 1938) was demolished and in March 1993 the new Umbro Stand was opened. Finally, on 3 April 1994 the old Kippax Terrace (which had been roofed originally in 1956) was closed; the new £11 million Kippax Stand was opened in November 1995. Before its closure, Main Road provided fans with a 33,500 all-seated capacity. With the club's playing fortunes taking a nose-dive — playing one season in the Second Division before two successive promotions and one more relegation — there was no

immediate impetus to fulfil the earlier proposals to rebuild the remainder of the ground in a style similar to the Kippax Stand in order to achieve a 45,000-seat capacity despite a return to the Premiership. In place of further possible development at Maine Road, the club agreed that, from the start of the 2003/04 season, it would relocate to the new stadium being built in the city to host the 2002 Commonwealth Games at Eastlands. As planned, the club moved into the new City of Manchester Stadium, with its 48,000-seat capacity, at the start of the 2003/04 season.

Below: 2004 (697228)
Right: 1923 (9271)

98

Manchester United

Then: 21 September 1965
Now: 1 May 2001

With its current capacity of around 68,000 all-seated, Old Trafford is by far the biggest ground in the Premiership and, if United progress their future schemes, this capacity could increase to some 75,000 in total. Although Manchester United — as Newton Heath — was first founded in 1878 and joined the Football League in 1892, it was not until 19 October 1910 that the club played its first game at the ground with which it has become synonymous. The new ground, designed by the ubiquitous Archibald Leitch, comprised a multi-span Main Stand and open banking, with corner terraces, on the remaining three sides. The first of these two views shows Old Trafford being modernised during the mid-1960s when the original cover on the United Road (North) Side was replaced by the new United Road Stand; this opened in August 1965 and provided seats for 10,000 and 55 executive boxes. As can be seen work is not yet completed in September 1965 on the corner cover. Opposite the United Road Stand is the Main Stand; this was rebuilt in 1950/51 after wartime damage (which resulted in United playing at Maine Road between 1941 and 1949). The corner stand covers are the original covers provided in the 1920s; these were undamaged by the bombing of World War 2. The Stretford End had been covered in 1959 and, three years later, seating was installed at the rear of the stand.

The scene at Old Trafford is very different today. However, this change has been the result of evolution over a number of years rather than the panic resulting from the necessity to become all seater which has affected other major grounds. The first change after the 1966 World Cup came in 1973 when the United Road Stand was extended round and over the then uncovered Scoreboard End. Two years later the executive suite was built behind the Main Stand and over the road that ran behind it. To ensure visibility from the executive suite and ancillary areas, the Main Stand roof was progressively rebuilt between 1975 and 1984. In 1987, with the floodlighting now attached to the stand covers, the existing pylons were removed. In 1990 the lower section of the United Road Stand was seated and the following year saw the seats in the Main Stand replaced. In May 1992 the Stretford End terrace closed and was demolished; the first section of the new stand opened in September 1992 with the remainder being completed in mid-1993. The stadium became all-seater in August 1994 when the final section of the Scoreboard End was fitted. The next phase in the development saw the rebuilding of the United Road Stand, extended at the back over land acquired from the Trafford Park industrial estate, in 1995/96. In 1999 work started on the construction of the second tier of the East (Scoreboard) End with the intention of adding a further 6,000 seats to the ground's capacity and this work was then followed by the construction of a second tier at the West (Stretford) End, which took Old Trafford's capacity to over 67,000 by the end of the 2000/01 season. Whilst the club would like to expand the South Stand, there are practical reasons why that is difficult; as a result, the club is focusing its attention on in-filling the Northeast and Northwest corners to create a stadium with a 75,000 capacity. There is, as yet, no timescale for this work.

Left: 1965 (A152731)
Far left: 2001 (688587)

Mansfield Town

Then: 2 June 1963
Now: 28 February 2002

Although Field Mill was a long-established sports venue, it was not until April 1919 that Mansfield Town moved there. The club had been formed as Mansfield Wesleyans in 1897, becoming Mansfield Town in 1910. The club joined the Midland League in 1922 and in 1931 was admitted to the Football League. The earlier of the two photographs shows part of the ground in 1963, shortly after the introduction of floodlights in 1961; ironically, in 1930 Field Mill had been the venue for one of the first experiments in the use of floodlights but it was another 30 years before the ground possessed a permanent set. The ground shows evidence of much of the work undertaken over the 40-year period. The curved frontages to the terraces at the North (covered in 1956) and South terraces are evidence that, between 1929 and 1932, Field Mill played host to greyhound racing. The Bishop Street Stand was constructed in 1939 and replaced a slightly older cover built in 1928. When the Bishop Street Stand was constructed, the old West Stand, illustrated here, reverted to terracing with its benches transferred to the new stand. In 1966 the old West Stand was replaced by a new construction, although the replacement stand was acquired second-hand from a race course at Hurst Park, near Hampton Court, where it had been originally constructed in 1937.

Today, Field Mill is radically different. Although the club had investigated the possibility of relocation, in the event it was decided to rebuild the existing ground, with work commencing in 1999/00 with the demolition of the Quarry Lane and North ends and their replacement by two 2,200-seat stands. This work was completed in early 2001. Attention then turned to the reconstruction of the 1966-built West Stand; this was completed by the end of the 2000/01 season and was to be followed by the rebuilding of the Bishop Street Stand with the intention of converting Field Mill into a ground with a 10,000 all-seated capacity. This phase of the ground's rebuilding has, however, yet to be completed and there is no confirmed timescale for the work.

Below: 1963 (A113663)
Right: 2002 (692625)

Middlesbrough

Then: September 1971
Now: 13 June 2004

The history of football in Britain has been littered with clubs that have gone into liquidation and have, at the last moment, been rescued. Such a case in point is Middlesbrough; few of those who witnessed the team's first 'home' games in 1986/87 — played at Hartlepool — would have believed that less than a decade later the team would be playing at a new £12 million stadium — the Cellnet Riverside Stadium.

For more than 80 years, Middlesbrough's home was at Ayresome Park and the first of these two photographs shows the ground in the early 1970s, shortly after the installation of the roof over the terracing at the East End. The club was established in 1876 and joined the Football League in 1899. The first game at Ayresome Park was played on 1 September 1903. The ground illustrated here shows the Main (North) Stand built in 1903 to the designs of Archibald Leitch. The South Stand was built in 1936/37 and replaced the earlier structure which had been moved from the team's earlier ground at Linthorpe Road. Also just prior to the outbreak of World War 2, the Holgate (West) End was provided with a cover. Floodlighting was installed in 1957 and the East End was covered in 1965/66 at which time additional seating was installed under the new roof as well as in the North Stand paddock.

Although the club was faced with turning Ayresome Park into an all-seater stadium, a proposed relocation meant that this work was never completed. A take-over of the club by Steve Gibson meant that those within the club who wished to see the club remain at Ayresome Park were defeated and plans for the new stadium were

unveiled in July 1994. The last league game was played at Ayresome Park on 30 April 1995. The first game at the new Cellnet Riverside Stadium was played on 26 August 1995. As originally built, the Riverside Stadium was provided with linked North, South and East stands and a separate West Stand, in which the club's offices were housed. The new ground provided an all-seater capacity of just under 30,000. Such has been the success of the team in generating support — despite fluctuating fortunes on the pitch — that in mid-1998 work started on the construction of the infill stands between the West and the North and South stands. This work took the capacity at the Riverside Stadium to 35,100. The club has long-term plans for the construction of extra tiers on the North, South and East stands in order to increase capacity ultimately to 42,000, although there is no time scale for this work at the current time.

Below: 2004 (697423)
Right: 1971 (A220141)

Millwall

Then: 1993
Now: 15 June 2004

Founded on the Isle of Dogs (north of the River Thames) in 1885, it was not until 22 October 1910 that Millwall migrated south of the river and played its first game at The Den. At that date the ground consisted of three open terraces and a Main Stand designed by Archibald Leitch. Ten years after moving to The Den, Millwall joined the Football League.

The first of these two photographs was taken at the point that the club moved from The Den to its new stadium. Although there have been a number of cases where local authorities have thwarted the efforts of clubs either to modernise existing grounds or to relocate to new stadia, in the case of Millwall, Lewisham Council proved highly co-operative. The original ground was, as noted above, originally built with one Main Stand and three open terraces. During the late 1930s, covered accommodation was provided at the rear of the three open sides. However, during one fateful week in 1943, the ground suffered severe damage. Firstly, a bomb attack saw the cover over the North Terrace destroyed whilst, a week later, a fire caused by a cigarette caused severe damage to the Leitch-designed Main Stand. Millwall was forced temporarily to vacate the ground — playing its games for a period at Charlton's Valley ground. The wartime damage took a number of years to repair completely, although Millwall's exile was relatively short-lived. Floodlighting was first installed in 1953 and in 1962 the Main Stand was fully seated and reroofed. The last major change came at the original ground in 1985 when an extension was built to the North Terrace roof to provide a new family section.

The major impetus for redevelopment at Millwall came with the club's success in reaching the old First Division — ironically the last London league team to achieve that status — when it was faced with making the ground all-seater. While it would have been practical (if expensive) to have rebuilt the original ground, the decision was taken to build a brand new stadium. The original ground was sold to a housing company, Fairview Homes, and on 8 May 1993 Millwall played its last game at its home for more than 80 years. The new ground, designed by the Miller Partnership, is provided with stands on all four sides; the total, all-seater, capacity is 20,150. The first game played at the new ground was a friendly against Sporting Lisbon on 4 August 1993. To emphasise the link between council and club, a council-run sports centre is located behind the North Stand. The new ground has not been without controversy (not least over its name); unusually, the club placed the actual management of the stadium in the hands of a management company with the intention of using the facility for other — non-football — events, such as pop concerts. In reality, this has proved less successful and the arrangement with the management company later ceased.

Right: 1993 (620290)
Far right: 2004 (697387)

Milton Keynes Dons

Then: 5 May 1961
Now: 9 February 2004

There are few more remarkable stories in English football than the rise of Wimbledon, as Milton Keynes Dons were known until June 2004, from non-league status in 1977 to the old First Division in 1986 and to FA Cup winners two years later. The self-styled 'Crazy Gang' proved that it was still possible to rise through the Football League to the top; ironically, however, if the club had joined the Football League a decade later, it is unlikely that the club's rise would have been so rapid. With success, however, came the realisation that Plough Lane, the club's home since 1912, would never meet the requirement to become all-seater. As a result, in May 1991 Wimbledon played its last first team game there — the ground remained for a time for reserve and youth games — and from the start of the 1991/92 season moved to share with Crystal Palace at Selhurst Park. The supposedly short-term arrangement in southeast London has proved longer than the club — and its long-suffering fans — would appreciate, as schemes for relocation either within the London Borough of Merton or elsewhere came to nothing.

The first of these two photographs shows Plough Lane in the early 1960s, immediately before the club turned professional in 1964. At this time, through the generosity of Sydney Black, the ground had developed significantly. Work at this time included the construction of the Main (North) Stand in 1958, the building of the Sportsman Pub at the ground's northwest corner also in 1958, the construction of a cantilevered roof over the East Terrace in 1959 and the installation of floodlights in 1960. Apart from these facilities, the ground was also provided with a South Stand; this had been acquired second-hand from the Millfields Road ground of Clapton Orient in 1923 and had been refurbished in 1950. Plough Lane was to survive in a peculiar half life for a decade, not being demolished until 2002.

For the full story of Selhurst Park, see Crystal Palace on pp58/59. In the decade since the Dons moved to southeast London there have been a number of schemes to relocate, both back to Wimbledon or elsewhere (including, bizarrely, a proposal to move lock, stock and barrel to — Dublin!). Following years of uncertainty — and increasing financial worries that led the club into Administration in 2003 — the FA finally agreed to allow the club to relocate to a temporary home at the National Hockey Stadium at Milton Keynes.

This decision was not backed by many of the club's fans, who established a rival team — AFC Wimbledon based at Kingstonian — that is gradually climbing the non-league pyramid. The move to Milton Keynes was delayed until after the start of the 2003/04 season whilst temporary stands, costing £2.5 million, were constructed at the stadium, taking the ground's capacity to 9,000. With a new consortium seeking to take the club forward, there are ambitious plans for the construction of a new 28,000-seat stadium at Denbigh Hall, funded as part of a retail development. This new ground is planned for completion by 2006. In late June 2004 it was announced that the FA were permitting the club to change its name to reflect its new location.

Right: 2004 (696928)
Below: 1961 (A87211)

Newcastle United

Then: 7 May 1961
Now: 31 March 2003

Newcastle United has been based at St James's Park for more than a century, but its relationship with its landlords — the council and freemen of the city — has not always been happy, particularly as the council has historically thwarted many of the club's proposals for the redevelopment of the ground. The results of this can be seen all too readily in the first of these two photographs where, even in the early 1960s, the ground is provided with covered accommodation on only two sides.

The club, which was to become Newcastle United in 1893 (the same year in which it joined the Football League), was established as East End in 1881. It inherited St James's Park from the collapsed West End in 1892; West End was not the first club to have played in the vicinity as an earlier team, Newcastle Rangers, dated from 1880. The ground as illustrated here in 1961 was the result of two phases of development work. The Main Stand was constructed in 1905; although, with the central gable, the work is reminiscent of the work of Archibald Leitch, he was not involved at this time. Leitch, however, was influential in the mid-1920s when he drew up a plan for the development of the ground; in the event only the Leazes Park End was covered in 1930 as further proposals for redevelopment were rejected by the council. Floodlighting was installed in 1953 initially. Shortly after the date of this photograph, frustrated by the problems with getting approval for redevelopment, United seriously contemplated relocation to Gosforth Park; in the event this was not progressed and eventually permission was granted to redevelop at St James's.

The first phase of the redevelopment occurred between 1971 and 1973 when the 3,400-seat East (Leazes Terrace) Stand was constructed. In 1977 the existing roof over the Leazes Park End was removed; the plan was for the construction of a new stand, but in the event this was not actually completed until 1993 (this is now the Sir John Hall Stand). After the Bradford fire of 1985, the Main Stand was eventually condemned and, after a number of temporary measures, was to be demolished in August 1987; the new Jackie Milburn (West) Stand replaced it. The new stand opened in 1990. The slow progress of the redevelopment of the ground was partly the result in the slump in the club's playing fortunes and partly the result of the debts incurred in earlier work. The result of both was a long-standing campaign by John Hall and his 'Magpie' group to take over; this was finally achieved in 1992. Apart from the Sir John Hall Stand, the new consortium has also overseen the construction of the new Gallowgate Stand (replacing the Gallowgate Terrace) which opened, with the corner stand in the southeast in 1994. The southwest corner stand, opened the following year.

Initially, the modernised St James's Park had a capacity of 37,000 all-seated. But this was a great deal smaller than the club required and there were controversial proposals to relocate to a new stadium on a greenfield site at Castle Leazes where a new 55,000-seat stadium would have been built. However, these plans were abandoned in favour of further redevelopment work at St James's Park to increase capacity to more than 50,000. Work started on the expansion of the Sir John Hall and Millburn stands along with the connecting Northwest Stand in 1998 with work being completed during the 2000/01 season. This work added a further 15,000 seats to St James's Park's capacity, making a total of 52,000 in all. Theoretically, the next phase in any redevelopment of the ground would involve the Gallowgate End and the East Stand, but there are potential problems with both sites and the club has no immediate plans for further development with the completion of the current work.

Left: 1961 (A87461)
Below: 2003 (694853)

Northampton Town

Then: 8 July 1968
Now: 9 February 2004

Widely regarded as perhaps the worst ground in the Football League during the surveys of football grounds in the immediate aftermath of 1985 Act, the reasons for the County Ground's lack of a fourth side is all too apparent in this mid-summer view of July 1968 — the site of the 'missing' side was required to allow for the playing of cricket. The use of the County Ground by Northamptonshire County Cricket Club dates to the mid-1880s, a decade before the football club was established in 1897. Town were to join the Football League in 1920. The ground as portrayed here was the result of Town's miraculous ascent to the old First Division in the early 1960s (a pinnacle that it occupied for only one season, 1962/3). The Main Stand dated from 1924 (replacing an earlier structure dating from 1907), which was repaired after fire damage in 1929. As early as the 1930s there was talk of relocation, but this had come to nothing. The Hotel End was roofed in 1951 and, in order to increase capacity for the First Division, additional open terracing was added to the existing Kop. This extension can be clearly seen on the right of the ground. Following the survey of the ground, the capacity was dramatically reduced. In March 1992 the club went into Administration, but was to recover. However, at the end of the 1993/94 season, Town finished last and it was only as a result of the fact that Kidderminster Harriers' ground failed to meet League standards that Town survived in the League. By this date, however, work had already started on the construction of the new Sixfields Stadium; delays meant that the 1994/95 season started at the County Ground, where the last game was played on 11 October 1994. The first game at the new ground took place on 15 October 1994.

The new ground was designed by the architects Taylor, Tulip & Hunter and cost £5.25 million. Of this, the bulk came from the local authority (largely as a result of the sale of its local bus company) and the remainder (£1 million) from the Football Trust. Town are tenants of the new stadium, which is designed as a community facility for other events and, as can be seen, one of the stands (the East) is double-sided providing accommodation for the adjacent athletics track. The two end stands — North and South — accommodate 971 each, whilst the West Stand seats 3,955 and the East Stand 1,756. During the 2003/04 season the club changed hands and the new owners announced plans to expand the Sixfields Stadium to a 16,000-seat capacity. There is, however, no timescale confirmed at present.

Right: 1968 (GF1856)
Below: 2004 (696949)

112

Norwich City

Then: 12 September 1961
Now: 18 May 2004

Although Norwich City was founded in September 1902 and joined the Southern League as a professional team three years later, it was not until 1935 that the club moved into Carrow Road. From 1908 until 1935, when the ground was condemned, City played at the Nest. The Carrow Road site was owned by Colmans and occupied as a sports ground by Boulton & Paul. On 1 June 1935 the latter agreed to sublet the ground to City and 10 days later work commenced. By the time that the first game was played on 31 August 1935 the ground was already well developed, with a 3,500-seat Main Stand and three open embankments. The 'Then' view shows the ground in the early 1960s, by which date the Station End had been covered (1937; being renamed the Barclay End), floodlights had been installed in October 1956 and the terrace opposite the Main Stand had also been covered (in 1960/61); this latter area was renamed the South Stand after Arthur South. Today, Carrow Road is radically different. Part of the original South Stand received seating in 1975 with the remainder being converted in 1992. In December 1979 the uncovered River End was replaced with the River End Stand. On 25 October 1984 the centre section of the Main Stand was destroyed by fire; this resulted in the closure of the whole stand and its replacement by the new 3,100-seat City Stand which opened in August 1986. This was followed in April 1992 by the demolition of the old Barclay End and its replacement by a new £2.8 million stand, which opened in August that year. Also in 1992, the lower tier of the River End Stand was fitted with seats. Two years later the City Stand was linked to the Barclay Stand with a small corner stand; a similar structure linking the City Stand to the River End Stand was completed in 1995. The next phase came with the redevelopment of the South Stand, initially proposed in 1995. The original stand was demolished in May 2003 to allow for the construction of a single-tiered 8,000-seat capacity stand costing £6.5million with 1,500 in-fill seats. The first phase of the stand was opened on 31 January 2004 with the complete structure being opened by the end of the 2003/04 season. The club has plans, allowed for in the construction of the new stand, to construct a second tier on the stand, adding a further 4,000 to Carrow Road's new capacity of 24,500. With promotion to the Premiership in May 2004 work started on the infill between the South and River End stands to add a further 1,600 seats. This is due for completion in March 2005. There are also plans to add a further tier in the long term to the Main (Geoffrey Watling) Stand, increasing the ground's capacity to 35,000. However, there is no timescale for these future developments and much, probably, depends on the club retaining its new-found Premiership status beyond the 2004/05 season.

Right: 1961 (A95780)
Inset: 2004 (697223)

115

Nottingham
Forest

Then: 31 July 1969
Now: 28 February 2002

Although initially Nottingham Forest were overshadowed by their near neighbours Notts County, recent years have seen widely differing fortunes for the two teams, with Forest now in the League Championship (after a short period in the Premiership) and County in League Two. Nottingham Forest were founded in 1865, gaining the club name from the Forest Recreation Ground; after an itinerant life, the club moved to the future City Ground in 1898, playing their first game there on 3 September 1898. By that date, Forest had already turned professional (1889) and had been admitted to the Football League (1892). The first of these two photographs shows the City Ground in the late 1960s, immediately after the fire which had damaged the Main Stand (on 24 August 1968). The fire did not seriously damage the roof of the building, and a new Stand was recreated beneath it. Opposite the Main Stand is the East Stand, which was constructed in 1957. Alongside the river is the covered Trent End; this structure was the result of an enlargement in 1954 of an older roof. The opposite end — the Bridgford End — remained uncovered terracing, having been extended during the 1950s. Although there were proposals — promoted by the City Council (which owns the City Ground) — for both of the Nottingham clubs to relocate, Forest chose to modernise the City Ground. Apart from the old Main Stand, which is still extant, all the other three sides have been rebuilt. The first to change was the East Stand, which was replaced by the Executive Stand in 1980. This was followed in 1992 by the Bridgford Stand; the curious roof line of this structure is the result of the club accommodating the concerns of the local residents. Finally, the Trent End Stand which was completed in 1994. The next phase in any development is likely to be the reconstruction of the Main Stand to increase the ground's capacity to 40,000, although this will not be undertaken until the club has achieved promotion back to the Premiership and acquired the freehold of the stadium.

Left: 1969 (A198143)
Below: 2002 (692565)

Notts County

Then: 31 July 1969
Now: 28 February 2002

Founded originally in 1862, the year before the Football Association, and a founder member of the Football League in 1888, County can lay claim to being one of the most historically important clubs in England. After leading a nomadic existence, County settled in to Meadow Lane in 1910, playing their first game there on 3 September 1910. The ground at this stage was provided with a Main Stand, a banked north end that formed a Kop, a small (1,400-seat) stand at the Meadow Lane End (which had followed the club from Trent Bridge) and a cover along the Tinkers Brook Side. As can be seen from the 'Then' photograph, little had changed by the late 1960s with the exception of the construction of the County Side Stand in 1925 when Tinkers Brook had been put into a culvert. Floodlights had been originally installed in 1953, but had been improved in 1962. The real changes to Meadow Lane are all too readily visible when examining the more recent photograph. Change has been the order of the day, as Meadow Lane was converted into a 20,300 all-seater stadium. The first stage of this work saw the demolition of the old Trent Bridge stand in 1978; the site was largely used to build the Meadow Club and, until the late 1980s when a small (750-seat) terrace was constructed, there was no accommodation at this end for supporters. The most dramatic change was, however, to be announced in January 1992 when the club reported that it intended to rebuild three sides of the ground for the start of the 1992/93 season. The work, which cost some £3 million (a staggeringly small amount in comparison with other work elsewhere), saw the building of a Family Stand backing on to the Meadow Club (replacing the small terrace of the late 1980s), the Kop Stand (seating 5,438 and replacing the Tinkers Brook Side) and the Jimmy Sirrel Stand (seating 2,283 and replacing the open terrace at the North End). The final piece of Meadow Lane's redevelopment came in 1994 with the rebuilding of the 1910 Main Stand; the last game played in front of it took place on 30 April 1994 and by August 1994 a new £4 million Main Stand — named after Derek Pavis (the chairman who had masterminded the ground's dramatic change) — with its 6,084 seats was ready.

Below: 2002 (692580)
Right: 1969 (A198148)

Oldham
Athletic

Then: 22 August 1968
Now: 18 May 2004

Founded as a pub team (Pine Villa) in 1897, the future Oldham Athletic (the name was changed in 1899) took over at Boundary Park when the earlier professional team, Oldham County, collapsed in 1899. For 1899/00 the new Athletic played at Boundary Park — where County had played the first game on 19 September 1896 — but then moved away, only returning in 1906. In 1907 Oldham were admitted to the Football League, at which time Boundary Park was provided with two stands: the Main (Sheepfoot Street) Stand and the Broadway (or Flat) Stand. The former was rebuilt in 1913 and this structure still forms the core of the current Main Stand. These two structures are clearly evident in the 'Then' photograph, along with the covered Chadderton Road End (covered — at the second attempt — in 1928) and the floodlights which were first installed in 1961. Although not visible here, during the 1960s — when a certain Ken Bates was chairman — executive boxes were installed in the paddock in front of the Main Stand. The contemporary Boundary Park is still reminiscent of the ground of 30 years ago; the Broadway Stand was rebuilt in 1971 and today accommodates some 2,666 seated fans spilt between a covered stand and an open paddock. The Chadderton Road End was reprofiled and reclad in 1991 at which time seating was also installed; it currently holds 3,634. The Main Stand, largely unchanged from the older structure (although its roof has been extended over the previously open paddock), now accommodates just under 2,400. Finally, the Rochdale Road Stand, replacing the open terrace, was built over the existing banking in 1992; the £1.95 million structure provides seating for just under 4,700. The club announced in mid-1998 that it intended to build a completely new stadium adjacent to the existing ground with the intention that the new ground would be complete for the start of the 2000/01 season; in the event, however, this scheme was abandoned in favour of a proposal to build a 15,000-seat ground in conjunction with the town's Rugby League team adjacent to the A627. This new scheme also fell by the wayside and the club decided in mid-2000 to develop further Boundary Park. The first phase of the redevelopment will be the construction of a new two-tier stand, costing £15 million, to replace the existing Lookers Stand. However, there is new confirmed time-scale for this work at present. Currently, Boundary Park has an all-seated capacity of just over 13,500.

Left: 2004 (697193)
Below: 1968 (A189942)

121

Oxford United

Then: 1992
Now: 14 February 2002

When the first edition of this book was published in 1998, the new Oxford United Ground at Minchery Farm was described as 'Future' rather than 'Now'. Between the first and second editions of the book, work eventually progressed to the point where the team could move. Thus, after some six years, Oxford United finally achieved its long-term desire of relocating from the cramped and dated Manor Ground.

The future Oxford United was founded as Headington in 1893 and, after a number of moves (including earlier spells at the Manor Ground), finally settled at the Manor Ground in 1925; the ground had seen its first game on 1 October 1898. In 1949 Headington turned professional, entering the Southern League; the club became Oxford United in 1960 and joined the Football League in 1962 (at the expense of Accrington Stanley). The piecemeal development of the Manor Ground is all too evident from this view taken in the era immediately after the club's glory years in the old First Division. The Main Stand, some 50yd in length is on the Beech Road side; this was built in 1955-57 and provided facilities previously housed in the small stand (built in 1949) to its left. The wedge-shaped Cuckoo Lane End was created in 1962-65 as a result of the club's admission to the Football League, as was the covered London Road End (in 1963; this work was contemporaneous with the installation of the floodlighting pylons although the Manor Ground had played floodlight games as early as 1950). The two small stands on the Osler Road Side were completed in 1984/85 as a result of United's promotion to the First

Division; the adjacent covered terrace was also upgraded at this time. With a capacity of less than 10,000 (of which only 60% could sit), the Manor Ground was living on borrowed time.

On 7 June 1995 it was announced that United would move to a brand new, 15,000 all-seater stadium on the outskirts of the city. Work started with the intention of having the ground completed for the 1997/98 season; in the event, work was suspended in mid-1997 and it was to be a further three years before work was restarted on the new ground. The new ground, named the Kassam Stadium after the club's chairman, opened with the start of the 2001/02 season. Initially it was provided with only three stands and has a current capacity of some 12,500; whilst the club has plans for the construction of the missing West stand, there is no definite timescale at present. Since the club moved, permission was granted in 2002 for the redevelopment of the Manor Ground, and the old ground has now disappeared under a housing and hospital development.

Below: 1992 (614428)
Right: 2002 (692175)

Peterborough United

Then: 24 October 1971
Now: 17 May 2004

Known as 'Posh', Peterborough United were relatively recent recruits to the Football League, replacing Gateshead in 1960. Although the club itself was founded only in May 1934, London Road had been used for sporting activities since the early years of the 20th century. When Peterborough United were formed, the only facilities at the ground were a small 400-seat stand. The bulk of the developments illustrated in the 'Then' photograph date from the 1950s, when Posh were one of the most successful non-league teams in the country. In 1951 part of the London Road End received a roof. From 1955 until 1958 there were almost constant changes. A new main stand was built between 1955 and 1958 and, when completed, the pitch was moved 20yd to the east following demolition of the original stand. Other work included the covering of the Moys End terrace and the construction of terracing parallel to Glebe Road. In the mid-1960s the roofs over the London Road End and the Moys End were extended; the extensions can be clearly seen in the changed colours of the roofing at both ends.

In the 30 years since the 'Then' photograph was taken, there have been further developments at London Road. A number of these were in response to the 1985 Act, which had temporarily resulted in the ground's capacity being slashed to 9,000. The major change was the construction of the 4,700-seat Freemans' Family Stand which replaced the old Glebe Road Terrace and which opened in March 1996; the cost was some £1.36 million. The Main Stand is now seating throughout, following the insertion of seats into the old Paddock; the stand's capacity is 4,950. During the summer of 1999 the club spent £40,000, working on both the Moys Terrace and London Road Terrace. The work included the reroofing of both sections. Today London Road has a capacity of over 15,000 and United is planning to develop further the ground. Work on the Main Stand is likely to be first, with redevelopment also to be undertaken on both the London Road and Moys ends, although the time-scale is uncertain.

Right: 2004 (697316)
Far right: 1971 (A220537)

Plymouth Argyle

Then: 6 September 1967
Now: 14 February 2002

Arguably one of the best located of all the traditional football stadia in Britain, Home Park is situated in a location with ample parking and other sporting facilities. The ground's origins date back to the early 1890s when it was first used for rugby; in 1901 it was occupied by the Argyle Athletics Club. With the rise of professional football, the club, which had run a football team, decided to gauge the potential interest for professional football in the town. A couple of trial matches proved popular and, on 5 September 1903, the first Southern League match was played at Home Park. At this time the ground was provided with two stands: a small stand (known as the Flowerpot or Spooner Stand) which was located where the open terrace at the west end of the Popular side is shown in the 1967 photograph; and a Main Stand (some 60yd in length) which dated from c1901. In 1920 Plymouth joined the Football League and 10 years later a new full-length Main Stand was constructed. At the same time, the terracing at the Devonport End was covered. However, the Main Stand was to be destroyed as a result of German bombing in 1941 and, at the end of the war, Home Park looked derelict. However, temporary repairs ensured that the ground was able to be used for the 1946/47 season.

The 'Then' photograph shows the development of the ground in the 20 years after the end of World War 2. Closest to the camera is the replacement Main Stand; this was built in 1952 to a double-deck design that harked back to the stands built in the 1930s and before. The Devonport End retained its prewar roof, but the Popular (or Lyndhurst) Side had been roofed in 1965. The Barn Park End — situated opposite the roofed Devonport End — had never been roofed and

remained an open terrace. The floodlights were installed in 1953 and were inaugurated officially in October of that year.

At the start of the new Millennium, Home Park had a capacity of just over 19,500. For a period in the late 1990s, the club was contemplating relocation to a new 25,000-capacity ground; however, this was abandoned in favour of reconstruction of Home Park. Work started on the redevelopment of the ground at the end of the 2000/01 season. The first phase of the work saw the demolition of the existing Lyndhurst, Devonport and Barn Park stands and the construction of a horseshoe-shaped stand in replacement. This new structure has a 12,700 all-seated capacity, taking the total capacity at Home Park to just over 20,000. The club has plans, but no confirmed timescale, for the replacement of the old Main Stand.

Left: 1967 (A175696)
Below: 2002 (692210)

Portsmouth

Then: 8 July 1957
Now: 25 February 2004

The story of Portsmouth and Fratton Park over the past decades evinces many of the problems that have afflicted the development of football grounds since the Bradford and Hillsborough disasters. Faced by a necessity to convert the ground to an all-seater format, the club was faced either by an historically confined site — which precluded major reconstruction — or by the fact that relocation would prove both expensive (and the club was not in a financial position to raise the necessary funds) and controversial. In the event, the club decided to reconstruct its facilities at Fratton Park, but only the extension to the requirement to become all-seater enabled these developments.

The first of these two photographs shows Fratton Park as it existed in the late 1950s, immediately after the Fratton End had been covered (in 1956). The club, founded in 1898, was based at Fratton Park from the start, where it played its first game on 6 September 1899. The ground as shown in this photograph shows both the South Stand — designed by Archibald Leitch and opened on 29 August 1925 (replacing an earlier structure) — and the North Stand — built in 1934-35 — to good effect. Unfortunately, the angle does not illustrate the mock Tudor building on Frogmore Street which provides Fratton Park with one of its more famous aspects. The floodlights at Fratton Park were installed in 1953 and, three years later, the ground played host to the first ever league game played under lights.

Today, Fratton Park is still recognisable as the ground that existed some 40 years ago, although with further developments planned this will inevitably change. Between 1989 and 1993, several million pounds was expended on upgrading the existing facilities, even though there were plans for relocation; in the event these plans came to nothing and Fratton Park was reprieved. In order to make the ground all-seater, both the paddocks on the north and south sides were fitted with seats in 1996 and the roof of the North Stand extended. Uncovered seating has also been installed at the Milton End. The major change has come at the Fratton End, where the original cover was demolished in 1988 and the terrace reduced; work started on the new Fratton Stand in 1997 and it was completed in 1998. This work resulted in the ground having covered accommodation on three sides and a capacity — all-seated — of 19,214. Initially, the club intended ultimately to complete the reconstruction of Fratton Park with the construction of a replacement stand at the Milton End; however, this was then abandoned in favour of a plan to build a new stadium on disused railway land to the west of Fratton Park. In the spring of 2003, a further revision saw the club propose redevelopment of Fratton Park once more. The new scheme envisages rotating the pitch by 90°, retaining the South Stand, the facade on Frogmore Road and the Fratton End, whilst constructing new stands to take the ground's capacity to 35,000 ultimately. The project, including residential developments and costing £125 million, was given local authority backing in late July 2004.

Above: 1957 (A68750)
Right: 2004 (697017)

Port Vale

Then: 29 June 1972
Now: 12 February 2002

Although in recent years football fans have become accustomed to the regular appearance of new ground, in the 40 years between the end of World War 2 and Scunthorpe United's move to Glanford Park only three teams — Hull City, Southend United and Port Vale — relocated. Promoted as the 'Wembley of the North', postwar austerity meant that the development of Vale Park was ultimately not quite as the original promoters intended.

The club's origins date back to before 1880, but the early years were not without their problems. In 1896 the club left the Football League, only to be readmitted in 1898. The original club went bankrupt in 1907 and its successor was only admitted back to the Football League in 1919 when it replaced Leeds City. In 1944 the site of the future Vale Park was acquired and, along with it, a scheme for a 70,000-seat stadium. The new ground — much more basic than that anticipated — was opened on 24 August 1950. The proposed Main Stand (on the Lorne Street Side) was not constructed; instead an open terrace surmounted by a small covered enclosure encompassed the players' access to the pitch. Opposite the Railway (West) Stand was constructed in 1954. The original proposals for Vale Park included a railway station on the adjacent railway line but this was never completed. The Bycars (North) End and the corner between it and the Railway Stand were covered, using the roof from the Swan Passage in Hanley, in 1950. The Bycars End was terraced eight years later in 1958. The fourth side was the open Hamil Road Terrace.

Vale Park has undergone some distinct developments over the past quarter century. Although the Lorne Street Side buildings have not changed, the Hamil Road End was provided with a cover in 1992 (using a roof acquired second-hand from Chester City; it had been installed new at Chester City's old Sealand Road stadium in 1979). Seats were installed in the Hamil Road End in 1995. The Railway Stand, which remains largely as it was in 1972, has been fitted with seats (in 1991). At the Bycars End, the original roof has been replaced — with the exception of the corner accommodation which has been converted into the Family Stand — following a fire in the mid-1980s. In the summer of 1998 Port Vale announced a plan for the redevelopment of Vale Park; this work involved

the construction of a new 5,000-seat stand in place of the Lorne Street Terrace. Work started on the new stand during the 1998/99 season with the demolition of the northern end of the existing Lorne Street side. The stand, as can be seen in the more recent photograph, is still incomplete; Vale's relegation from the First to Second Division at the end of the 1999/00 season means that the existing all-seated capacity of 20,000 is probably adequate at the current time although it will be a relatively quick job to complete the structure if necessary.

Far left: 1972 (A243358)
Left: 2002 (691728)

Preston North End

Then: 20 April 1972
Now: 1 March 2002

With the trend towards relocation, the number of grounds which could claim a long pedigree of continuous football has diminished. One of the exceptions to this trend is Deepdale which has been used for football since 1879 and which has been the home of Preston North End since 1875. North End — it became Preston North End slightly later — was founded as a cricket club in 1863 and moved to Deepdale 12 years later; the ground became football only in 1881. The first of these two photographs shows Deepdale as it was in the early 1970s. The oldest section of the ground's accommodation was the West Stand — on the right-hand side of the ground — which dates from January 1906. This was followed in 1921 by the Fulwood End Kop in 1921; this is the end closest to the camera. This was followed in the early 1930s by the construction of the covered Town End. In 1934 a 40yd-long stand — the Pavilion — was built on the east side of the ground; this was extended two years later by the South Pavilion. This meant that by the outbreak of war in 1939, Deepdale could provide covered accommodation on all four sides. The next development came in 1953 with the first installation of floodlights.

The changes at Deepdale over the past decade have been dramatic. In October 1994 local company Baxi took over the club and a process of redevelopment started. In May 1995 the old West Stand was demolished, to be replaced, in March 1996, by the new Tom Finney Stand. This, complete with face created out of seats, set the pattern for the next development of the ground. This new stage saw the demolition of the old Fulwood End and its replacement in 1998 with the new Bill Shankly Stand. Again, the new stand features a face created out of coloured seats. The third phase

of the rebuilding of Deepdale occurred during the 2000/01 season and involved the demolition of the covered terrace at the Town End — last used in March 2001 — and its replacement by a new stand. The new Stand — named the Alan Kelly Town End and incorporating a face from coloured seats as with the other two new stands — was opened in October 2001 and provides 6,100 seats taking the ground's current capacity to 22,225. The final phase of the ground's redevelopment will see a new stand constructed on the site of the existing Pavilion Stand and paddock, although there is no schedule for this work at present planning permission has been granted. Once completed, the ground's capacity will increase to 30,000.

Below: 2002 (692519)
Right: 1972 (A225838)

Queens Park Rangers

Then: 15 August 1928
Now: 16 June 2003

Although based at Loftus Road for more than 80 years, Queens Park Rangers dates back to a merger in 1886 between two teams (St Judes and Christchurch Rangers) and is a club that has led a somewhat nomadic existence. Even after moving to Loftus Road — where it played its first game on 8 September 1917 (although Shepherd's Bush had been playing there since 1904) — QPR has had two spells of playing at the now-demolished White City Stadium — in 1931-3 and 1962-3 — and in the mid-1960s there were plans to make the move permanent. This 'Then' shot is one of the oldest in the book and shows the ground as it existed in the late 1920s, shortly after QPR joined the Third Division in 1920. The ground was provided with three open terraces, whilst the fourth side — along Ellerslie Road — was provided with a cover in 1917 that had been transferred from QPR's previous ground at Park Royal. The foreground is dominated by the exhibition halls associated with the White City complex; these were to disappear in the 1930s. As can be seen the ground is in a confined location and this has led the club to contemplate the possibility — but no more than this at the current time — of relocation. The more recent photograph shows the results of the club's rebuilding programme from 1968 onwards. The first phase of this work saw the opening of the South Africa Road (North) Stand in 1968. This was followed in 1972 by the Ellerslie Road (South) Stand. The two-tier Loftus Road (East) End Stand was completed in 1980, with seats being fitted into the lower tier in 1994. Finally, in 1981, the School End was completed; this was further upgraded in 1993.

Today, Loftus Road has an all-seater capacity of 19,148 and, apart from QPR, wais also used for Rugby Union matches and, during two seasons from 2002 to 2004, it was also home to Premiership side Fulham. Although QPR's fall from grace was rapid — relegation from the First to Second Division at the end of the 2000/01 season although promotion at the end of 2003/04 results in League Championship football again — means that the existing capacity is probably adequate, it is not many years ago since QPR were a thriving Premiership team. In the event of the glory days being recaptured, the existing ground is too small to sustain a Premiership team and the site too confined to redevelop. As a result, the club has plans for a possible relocation, but nothing definite is confirmed at this stage.

Below: 1928 (22720)
Right: 2003 (695949)

Reading

Then: 11 August 1954
Now: 9 February 2004

Another of the traditional grounds that has disappeared over recent years is Reading's Elm Park, with the team moving into the new Madejski Stadium (at Smallmead to the south of the town) in late August 1998. Reading was founded in 1871 and played its first game at Elm Park on 5 September 1896. The club joined the Third Division in 1920. This 'Then' shot shows the ground in 1954 and shows the floodlights — first used in that year — but before the cover along the Tilehurst Road (Popular) Side was extended towards the Tilehurst End. The Main Stand opposite the Tilehurst Road Side dated from a rebuild of 1926. The first — central — section of the Tilehust Road Side had been covered in 1936; this was extended towards the Town End in the late 1940s.

From the mid-1980s Reading has led, at times, a somewhat controversial existence — witness Robert Maxwell's efforts to merge Reading with neighbouring Oxford United to form the Thames Valley Royals — and the slashing of the ground's capacity to 6,000 in 1985. Although work in 1985-6 saw the capacity increased again to 20,000, the threat of a much smaller all-seater capacity and the fact that Elm Park was in a confined space, led the club to start contemplating relocation. That this was possible was the result of John Madejski becoming chairman; having made his money with *Auto Trader*, Madejski turned his attention to his local football club. Plans were approved for a new stadium in 1996 and the new stadium, with its 24,200-seat capacity, is illustrated in the second view.

The new stadium was completed for the start of the 1998/99 season, although the team's relegation at the end of 1997/98 resulted in the Madejski Stadium staging Second, rather than First, Division football. In the three years since the ground's completion the surrounding area has become much more heavily developed (including the construction of a hotel linked to the West Stand) and the ground is now also home to London Irish RUFC. The club has plans, if the need arises, for the construction of a second tier, accommodating 5,000, on the East Stand.

Left: 1954 (R21116)
Below: 2004 (696940)

Rochdale

Then: 25 June 1955
Now: 23 February 2004

After a somewhat early chequered career in Rochdale, football finally became established in the town with the formation of Rochdale AFC in 1907. This was the third team in the town, following on from the first Rochdale AFC (1896-1901) and Rochdale Town (1902-3). The new club played its first game at Spotland — which had been used for Rugby since 1878 — on 3 September 1907. The club became a founder member of the Third Division (North) in 1921. The first of these two photographs shows the ground in the mid-1950s. The Main (South) Stand was built originally in 1921; as shown here it had just been repaired after a fire in August 1953 had slightly damaged one bay. Opposite the Main Stand is the Wilbutts Side Terrace; this was covered in part in 1927. On the east side is the Pearl Street End; this too was covered in the late 1920s. In 1948 the pitch, which previously had had a distinct slope, was levelled and the spoil was used at the Pearl Street End to create a Kop. The fourth side was, at this time, the uncovered Sandy Lane End. From August 1988 Rochdale Hornets RLFC moved to the ground and, between the football club, local council and rugby club, a partnership developed which has seen the ground considerably developed. The only other part of the 'old' Spotland to survive is the cover over the Sandy Lane End; this was constructed originally in 1961 but again reroofed in the 1980s. The floodlighting dates from 1992, replacing the earlier (1971) installation. Also in 1992, the new Main Stand was opened. This was followed in 1995 by the closure of the Pearl Street Stand; this was demolished and replaced by the new 2,700-seat WMG Stand, which was completed in 1998. The final phase in the redevelopment of Spotland occurred during 2000 when the Wilbutts Lane Terrace was demolished and the new 3,650-seat Willbutts Stand completed.

Right: 2004 (696973)
Far right: 1955 (A59813)

Rotherham United

Then: 1981
Now: 18 May 2004

Few grounds are located in such an area of heavy industry well away from centres of population as Rotherham United's Millmoor Ground, surrounded, as it is on two sides, by the scrapyard of C. F. Booth. The uncompromising location is all too evident in these two photographs which were taken 20 years apart. Rotherham County played its first game at Millmoor on 2 September 1907 having moved from an earlier ground (Red House) where the club had been established more than 20 years earlier as Thornhill. In 1919 Rotherham County were admitted to the Football League and, in 1925, merged with neighbouring Rotherham Town to form Rotherham United. The vertical shot was taken in 1981. Visible clearly are the Main Stand, the bulk of which dated back to 1920 and which was extended in 1964, and the 40yd-long Millmoor Lane Side cover (dating to 1928). The Railway End was covered in 1957 to be followed in 1968 by the Tivoli End. Floodlights were first installed in 1960. Although the more recent photograph was take from a different angle, it shows clearly that much of Millmoor is unchanged from the scene of 1981. The Main Stand is unchanged, as are the Tivoli and Railway ends. The Millmoor Lane side roof has been extended — the work was completed in 1982 — and more seats have been installed on this side. One factor is that initially Rotherham United contemplated relocation; however, the preferred site is no longer available and the club has decided to remain at Millmoor. Today, the capacity at the ground is 11,486, of which 6,949 are seated. There are proposals for the redevelopment of Millmoor — essential if United retains its League Championship status (achieved at the end of the 2000/01 season) — starting with the construction of a new Main Stand costing £4.25 million and providing seating for 7,000. There is, however, no timescale at present.

Left: 1981 (415406)
Below: 2004 (697157)

Rushden & Diamonds

Then: 18 September 1971
Now: 17 May 2004

One of the newest teams in the Coca Cola League — promoted at the end of the 2000/01 season in place of Barnet — was also one of the most ambitious teams to have emerged from the non-league structure in recent years — Rushden & Diamonds. However, the ambition demonstrated by this Northamptonshire-based team is of relatively recent origin and owes much to the backing of the man behind Doc Martens boots — Max Griggs. However, towards the end of the 2003/04 season, Griggs announced that he was seeking an exit strategy from the club and, following relegation from the Second Division at the end of the season, it would appear that the good times are perhaps over at Nene Park.

The two teams had very different origins. Rushden Town — whose ground is illustrated in the first of these two photographs — dated back to 1889 and by the late 1980s had progressed through the ranks of non-league football, reaching its apex in 1990/91 when the team played in the Premier Division of the Southern League. Despite finishing 14th and having upgraded its facilities at the Hayden Road ground in Rushden, it was deemed that the ground did not meet the league's standards and the team was relegated to the First Division. Irthlingborough Diamonds was a much more recent creation, first appearing in 1946. Initially a youth team, by the late 1960s Diamonds had entered the senior leagues. By the late 1980s, Diamonds had had considerable success in reaching the United Counties League and in FA Vase competitions. However, the club was not maintaining its progress until it started to approach local businessmen, including Max Griggs, for support. The result was the uniting of Rushden Town and Irthlingborough Diamonds, the new Rushden & Diamonds entering the Midland Division of the Southern League at the start of the 1992/93 season. The club progressed through the non-league pyramid to the Conference and, after a couple of seasons of near misses, finally achieved Nationwide League status in May 2001.

The first of these two photographs portrays Hayden Road in Rushden. The ground dates to 1922 and the Main Stand, as illustrated, also dates from that period. The photograph antedates the installation of floodlighting — which occurred in 1975-76 — but shows the Nissen Hut, installed in 1965, which was used as the clubhouse. This was destined to be replaced in the 1970s. Opposite the Main Stand is a small covered terrace between the football pitch and the cricket field.

The redevelopment of the original Irthlingborough Diamonds' Nene Park ground has been radical. Although Irthlingborough Diamonds was formed in the late 1940s, it was not until 1969 that it moved to the Nene Park site. The club quickly developed its new ground, providing covered seating for 350 and covered terraces for a further 1,000. Prior to the merger of the two teams, Nene Park's record crowd stood at some 2,400. However, the old Nene Park was to be swept away as the merged club's ambitions became evident. The first phase saw the construction of the 1,000-seat North Stand; this was completed in 1993-94. This work was followed by the construction of the Diamond Centre in 1994, the South Stand and the West (Peter de Banke) Terrace in 1994-95 and, finally, the East (Airwair) Stand in 1996. Today, Nene Park has a capacity of 6,553, of which 4,641 are seated.

Far right: 1971 (A216954)
Right: 2004 (697265)

Scunthorpe United

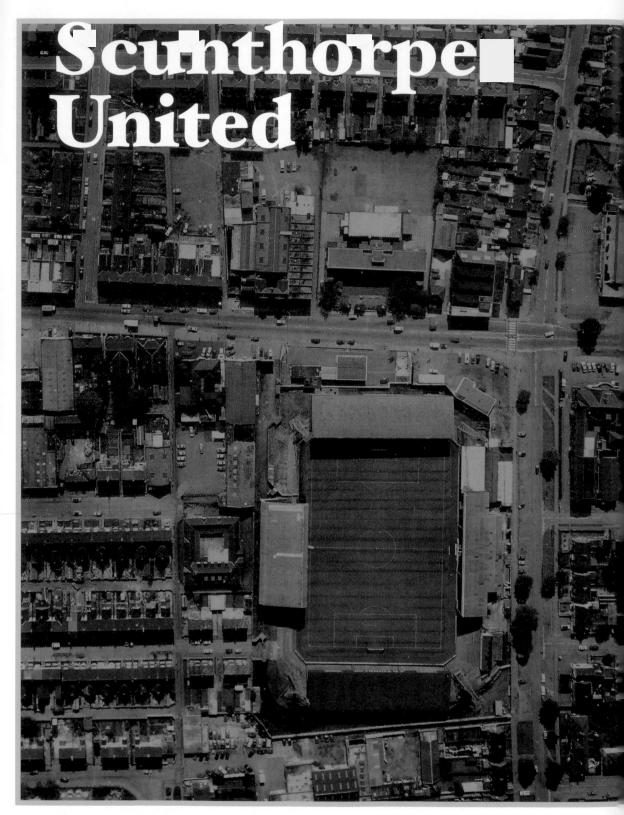

Then: 1983
Now: 13 June 2004

It is now more than a decade since Scunthorpe United moved into Glanford Park, playing their first game at the new stadium on 14 August 1988. In the 16 years since then, more than 20 new grounds have either been completed or are in development reflecting the great changes that have occurred in the face of football in England. These two photographs illustrate United's original ground just prior to its closure and demolition and the new ground. The Old Showground was first used for football in the mid-1890s. Scunthorpe United was formed by the union of earlier clubs in 1899; a further merger in 1910 with North Lindsey saw the club retitled as Scunthorpe & Lindsey United, a name which the club retained until 1956. United entered the Football League in 1950. The original ground as illustrated here was dominated by the East Stand; this structure was the result of a rebuild in 1958 after the original structure burnt down. When it opened on 23 August 1958, the East Stand was the first cantilevered structure at any football ground in Britain; unfortunately, despite its historic importance, this structure was demolished along with the rest of the Old Showground, after efforts to transfer it to the new ground proved impractical. Also visible in the first photograph are the covered Doncaster Road End (work undertaken in 1954) and the covered Fox Street End (this was undertaken in 1959 replacing a cover originally installed in 1938). Floodlighting was installed in 1957. The club played its last game at the Old Showground on 18 May 1988. The new ground provides covered accommodation on all four sides. Originally there were terraces at both ends, but the Caparo Merchant Bar End was fitted with seats in 1990. Today, the capacity at Glanford Park is 9,200, of which 6,400 are seated. Although the ground is relatively recent, there are plans that the Evening Telegraph Stand will be demolished and replaced with a new two-tier structure. There is, however, no timescale for this work.

Left: 1983 (448667)

Below: 2004 (697508)

Sheffield United

Then: 30 July 1951
Now: 18 May 2004

As with a number of other grounds, Bramall Lane developed alongside the cricket ground which predated it. Cricket was first played at Bramall Lane in the mid-1850s and it was not until the start of the following decade that football arrived. For a period the football side was occupied by Sheffield Wednesday, but it was not until Sheffield United was formed in September 1889 that the current occupants arrived. United, like Wednesday, became founder members of the Second Division of the Football League in 1892. Until the closure of the cricket ground — the cricket team was given to notice to leave in 1971 and the last County game was played at Bramall Lane on 7 August 1973 — the ground was, as is clearly shown in the 1951 photograph, three-sided. The Main Stand — along John Street — dated originally to 1902 when it represented Archibald Leitch's first commission outside Glasgow; it had been damaged by German bombing in 1940 and the damage was not to be completely repaired until 1954. The Shoreham Street End roof over the Kop dated back to 1935; this too had been damaged by German bombing but had been repaired in 1948. The Bramall Lane End had received a cover in 1905 at which time the John Street Stand roof had been extended. After the date of this photograph, floodlighting was installed in 1955; Bramall Lane did, however, have claim to fame — in 1878 it played host to the first game ever played under lights.

The changes at Bramall Lane have been dramatic. Although the club considered the possibility of relocation in the 1960s, this was not progressed and once the playing of cricket ceased, it was possible to turn Bramall Lane into a four-sided stadium. The £1 million South Stand was opened on 16 August 1975. The old John Street Stand was demolished in 1994 and work started on the replacement stand in March 1996; work was completed on the new stand in 1997. The Kop was to receive treatment in 1991; this included reroofing the structure and providing seats. The 1966-built Bramall Lane Stand was also converted to all-seater accommodation, with the upper tier being treated in 1994. The ground's current capacity is 30,936 and, with the completion of the John Street Stand, there are no further plans for major development at this stage other than for the construction of a corner stand with hotel between the Arnold Laver and Bramall Lane stands. There is, however, no timescale for this work.

Far right: 1951 (15249)
Right: 2004 (697170)

Sheffield Wednesday

Then: 30 July 1951
Now: 18 May 2004

As in Liverpool, one ground — in Sheffield's case Bramall Lane — has been used by two clubs. Wednesday were formed in 1867 and played at Bramall Lane occasionally (along with other grounds) before settling at Owlerton — from which name the club derives its nickname — in 1899. The first game at Owlerton was on 2 September 1899, seven years after the club had become a founder member of the Football League's Second Division. The impressive scale of Hillsborough is evident in the first of the two photographs, which dates to the early 1950s. Closest to the camera is the Main Stand; this was designed by Archibald Leitch and opened on 14 January 1914. Opposite the Main Stand was the stand moved from the previous Olive Grove ground and re-erected at Hillsborough in 1899. The short — but unconnected — extension was added in 1927. Also in 1927 the terrace at the Leppings Lane End was extended and the rear provided with a cover. Finally, the open Kop Terrace — the Penistone Road End — dated back originally to 1913.

Few football fans will need reminding that it was the tragic death of 95 Liverpool fans at Hillsborough — a 96th died later — during the FA Cup semi-final on 15 April 1989 that led to the Taylor Report of 1990 and to the determination that grounds should become all-seater.

Hillsborough today is dramatically different to the ground of 1951. The first stage in the ground's redevelopment occurred in 1961 when the old Olive Grove Stand was demolished. The new North Stand opened on 23 August 1961; it was the second cantilevered stand at any football ground in England and, with the loss of Scunthorpe's pioneering structure, is now the oldest to survive. The Leppings Lane Terrace was replaced by the two-tier West Stand; it was in the lower-tier of this that the April 1989 tragedy occurred. Following the tragedy, seating was installed in the lower tier and the roof extended in 1990-91. In 1986 the Kop End was provided with a roof; this was opened by HM the Queen on 12 December of that year. Seating was installed in the Kop during 1993. Although the core of the Main Stand remains that which Leitch designed — clearly evident through the frame of the roof — this was reroofed in 1992 and, more recently, the stand's external facade, which incorporates the club's offices, has been rebuilt. As a nice touch, the club incorporated a replica gable end — one of Leitch's trademarks — into the new roof. Today, Hillsborough has an all-seater capacity of 39,859.

Left: 1951 (R15259)
Below: 2004 (697178)

Shrewsbury Town

Then: 18 July 1961
Now: 13 June 2004

Delightfully situated on the banks of the River Severn, Gay Meadow has been the home of Shrewsbury Town since 1910. Although the club dates back to 1886, it had a number of alternative grounds before settling here. The first match played here was on 10 September 1910. The ground as illustrated in the 'Then' shot was very much the product of the prewar years. The Centre Stand, with its gable, was opened in October 1922. Between 1932 and 1937 the terrace at the Station (ie north) End was partially covered, as was the centre section of the Riverside Terrace between 1936 and 1939. The traditional scoreboard at the Wakeman (South) End was built in 1936. The final prewar development saw the construction of a second stand — the Station Stand — between the existing Centre Stand and the Station End. In 1950 Shrewsbury Town joined the Football League, when the league numbers were increased from 88 to 92, and in 1959 floodlighting was added. The extension of the Riverside Terrace roof to the north was completed during the 1950s.

The more recent photograph shows that there have been a number of developments over the past four decades. Firstly, the stands along the east side have been altered. In 1966 new offices were completed behind the Centre Stand. At the same time the Centre and Station stands were reroofed and a third stand — the Wakeman Stand — constructed at the south end; this final extension is marked by the different roof line. Although the main stand is effectively a single entity it is still referred to as being formed by the Wakeman, Centre and Station stands. Also the Riverside Terrace has had its roof extended southwards. Whilst not visible in this photograph, there have been further developments in the 1990s, with the improved seating in the stand.

As with a number of clubs, Shrewsbury Town has over the past few years been contemplating either relocation or redevelopment. Initially, it was relocation that was the preferred option; however, these plans were overturned in favour of reconstruction work at the Gay Meadow. Proposals were produced to convert the existing ground — with its 8,000 capacity of which 4,000 are seated — into an 18,000-capacity ground through the construction of new stands at the Station and Wakeman ends and the shifting of the pitch slightly to the north. More recently, however, the club has reverted to relocation, having identified a site at Oteley Road which it is hoping to develop with the local authority. If the scheme proposes, the club will construct a new 10,000-seat ground costing some £8.5 million. During the summer of 2001 an exercise in public consultation was undertaken in order to gauge support for relocation. However, whilst approval was gained for the new ground, problems over permission to redevelop the old Gay Meadow site resulted in delays, compounded by the team's relegation to the Conference at the end of 2002/03. A return to League Two at the end of 2003/04 has again brought the question of the new ground up the agenda, but there is still no confirmed timescale for any possible relocation.

Below: 1961 (A93733)
Right: 2004 (697453)

Southampton

Then: 17 May 1964
Now: 2 March 2002

The Dell, with an all-seater capacity of 15,250 and with a highly constrained site, was the smallest ground in the Premiership, with the result that the club endeavoured for many years to relocate. This ambition was finally achieved at the start of the 2001/02 season when the Saints moved to their new 32,000-seat ground. The club's origins date back to 1885 when a team was established by St Mary's YMCA — hence the club's nickname — and in 1894 joined the Southern League. The first game played at The Dell occurred on 3 September 1898 and in 1920 the club joined the Football League. The ground as illustrated in the first of these two photographs is very much the product of the period immediately after the club joined the league. Closest to the camera is the West Stand; this dated to 1928 and was designed by Archibald Leitch to replace an earlier structure. The West Stand was slightly damaged by fire during 1941. Opposite is the East Stand; this was constructed in 1929 after the old stand had been destroyed by fire on 4 May 1929. Floodlights were installed in 1951, the first League ground to receive them on a permanent basis. On the south side of the ground — on the Milton Road End — the club constructed three platforms, clearly visible here, which became known as the 'Chocolate Boxes'; these were unique in English football, being the only open-air upper-tier terraces in the country. The fourth end was the open-air Archers Road Terrace.

The West and East stands remained extant until the ground closed, although both were fitted with seating throughout; work to convert The Dell into an all-seater stadium was undertaken in 1993. Despite the confined area occupied by The

Dell, the club was able to provide seated accommodation at both the Milton Road and Archers Road ends. The first was to be completed was the Archers Road Stand in 1993; this was followed in 1994 by the Milton Road Stand (the 'Chocolate Boxes' had been demolished in 1981). Thus, The Dell fulfilled all the necessary requirements except one — its fundamental lack of capacity.

In the spring of 1999 the club was granted planning permission to construct a new all-seater stadium on Britannia Road. Sponsored by Friends Provident, the new St Mary's stadium, costing some £32 million, provides all-seater accommodation for some 32,000 and opened with the start of the 2001/02 season. The Dell bade farewell to football with a friendly against Brighton & Hove Albion — the first team to visit The Dell when it opened — and has subsequently been demolished to be replaced by a new housing development.

Left: 1964 (A128485)
Below: 2002 (692497)

Southend United

Then: 22 March 1968
Now: 17 May 2004

Until the opening of Scunthorpe United's Glanford Park ground in 1988, Southend United's ground at Roots Hall was the most recent ground in use in the Football League, seeing its first game on 20 August 1955. Ironically, however, this was the second time that the team had played at Roots Hall; it had left an earlier ground on the site in 1916 a decade after the club had been formed. Although the location was the same, the landscape had been altered considerably over the intervening years as a result of quarrying. The club first contemplated a return to Roots Hall in 1948, but it was not until March 1953 that work actually started. The first of these two photographs shows the ground as it appeared in the late 1960s. Facilities provided from the start included the short East (Main) Stand; this structure was extended in 1967 as illustrated here. On the North Terrace a short cover was installed from new; again this was subsequently extended as can be seen from the slightly lighter wing sections of the roof. On the West Side, a single roof was provided covering the rear of the terrace; this was again extended towards the pitch as shown here. The South Terrace was built over a five-year period between 1955 and 1960. Floodlighting was installed in 1959. As can be seen, Roots Hall still possesses its East Stand and covered North Terrace. The West Side has seen wings added (in 1995) to provide full cover the length of the pitch. The major change was the sale of the site of the South Terrace in 1988 and the construction of flats on the site; the old terrace was subsequently replaced by a narrow two-tier South Stand. Roots Hall is now all-seater — the West Side was provided with seats in 1991 and the North End in 1994 — with a current capacity of 12,392.

As part of the club's plans for relocation, Roots Hall was sold in the summer of 1999, although the club was initially granted a four-year period of grace before it had to vacate the ground (permission which has subsequently been extended to 2006 as a result in delays to its plans). Despite setbacks, the club is progressing with plans for a new 16,500-seat ground costing £12.5 million with the intention of moving by the start of the 2006/07 season. Whilst planning consent for the construction of the ground adjacent to the club's training facility at Fossetts Farm was rejected by the local authority in early 2001 the club has identified an alternative location.

Left: 1968 (A178467)
Right: 2004 (697287)

Stockport County

Then: 1994
Now: 15 May 2003

Another set of relatively recent comparisons shows the development of Stockport County's Edgeley Park ground during the mid-1990s. Founded as Heaton Norris Rovers in 1883, the club became Stockport County in the following decade. It moved to Edgeley Park — a ground used for rugby since 1901 — in 1902 and played its first game there on 13 September 1902. The ground as illustrated in 1994 shows the Main Stand, which had opened originally on 24 October 1936 in place of an earlier structure that had been destroyed by fire in 1935. Opposite the Main Stand is the Barlow (South/Popular) Side; this was named in 1956 after Ernest Barlow, at which time the surviving cover was added. Until 1978, this side stretched further back with a cover dating back to 1903. In 1985, as a result of concerns after the Bradford fire, the Cheadle (West) Stand was demolished and the 'Then' shot shows the situation prior to 1995 and the construction of the new Cheadle Stand as illustrated in the more recent view. At the same time as the Cheadle Stand was demolished, so the Railway (East) End open terrace was reduced in size. The earlier shot postdates the decision, taken in 1992, that the club would rebuild at Edgeley Park rather than seek to relocate. The following year, 1993, saw the Barlow (Vernons) Stand provided with seats. The major development here is the construction of the Cheadle End Stand; this £1.5 million structure was completed in August 1995 and provides accommodation for 4,800 seated fans. Edgeley Park's current capacity is 11,540 and the club's next phase of development will see the Railway End rebuilt as a 5,200-seat stand. Once this is completed, the club will turn its attention to upgrading the Vernon BS stand, although there is no timescale for any of this work. With Manchester City relocating away from Maine Road there were suggestions that County might relocate there rather than remain at Edgeley Park; these proposals, however, came to nothing. In 2003 County merged with the local Rugby Union side, Sale Sharks, with both teams now playing at Edgeley Park.

Right: 1994 (627691)
Far right: 2003 (695702)

Stoke City

Then: 1996
Now: 1998

With its good road connections and sizeable car parks, the Victoria Ground in Stoke, one of the oldest league grounds in England, was not an obvious candidate to be the victim of relocation, but that is exactly what happened in 1997 when Stoke City moved to its new ground, the Britannia Stadium. These two photographs, taken barely two years apart, show the Victoria Ground in its final form and the new stadium. The club's origins date back to the 1860s and then to a merger with the Stoke Victoria Athletic Club in 1878. The club played its first game at the Victoria Ground on 24 September 1883 before becoming a founder member of the Football League in 1888. The club left the League in 1890 only to be readmitted in 1891; a subsequent departure in 1908 was only reversed in 1919.

Examining the Victoria Ground first, the Main Stand was the result of a rebuilding scheme between 1960 and 1963 which replaced the original stand dating from 1922. The corner between the Main Stand and the two-tier Stoke End Stand (constructed in 1979) was originally a pavilion; this was rebuilt into a gym contemporaneously with the rebuilding of the Main Stand. Opposite the Main Stand is the covered Butler Street Side; the roof illustrated here was one installed in 1976 after the previous roof (installed in 1935 and extended over the corners in 1936) had been largely destroyed in a gale. The remaining part of the 1937 structure, adjacent to the Stoke End, was removed in 1983 and the old terracing left abandoned. The fourth side, the Boothen End was covered in 1930. At the time of the ground's closure, this was the largest remaining block of terracing in the Football League.

In March 1996 the go-ahead was given for the construction of the new stadium. This project, costing some £25 million, was completed in time for the 1997/98 season. The new ground, the Britannia Stadium, sponsored by the building society, has an all-seater capacity of 28,000. The club has long-term plans, but no timescale, to construct and in-fill stand between the Boothen End and the John Smiths Stand. This would take the ground's capacity to 30,000.

Below: 1996 (670087)
Right: 1998 (673545)

Sunderland

Then: 1992
Now: 1 May 2001

There are few places more redolent of footballing history than Sunderland's Roker Park, but, such is the increasing pressure within the game, even Roker Park could have no place in the all-seater future of British football. Sunderland was established in 1879 and joined the Football League in 1890. The club played its first game at Roker Park on 10 September 1898. The first of these views, taken in 1992, shows Roker Park as it existed in its latter days. Closest to the camera is the rear of the Clock Stand; this was rebuilt to a design of Archibald Leitch in 1936 replacing one of the original 1898-built stands. Opposite the Clock Stand is the Main Stand; this again was the work of Archibald Leitch and dated from 1929, being officially opened on 7 September of that year. Again it was a replacement for one of the original 1898 stands. To the left is the covered Fulwell End; this terrace had been expanded in 1925 and was to be covered in 1966 prior to Roker Park's use as a venue in the World Cup of that year. Other work in 1966 saw additional seating installed through the ground. By 1992 the only open area at Roker Park was at the Roker End; this had been constructed following Leitch's designs in 1911 but the rear section had been dismantled in 1982.

Whilst there were plans to turn Roker Park into an all-seater stadium, the club preferred to take the relocation option. A number of sites were investigated until the decision to relocate to the site of the closed Monkwearmouth Colliery was taken. This had ceased to produce coal in December 1993 and thus offered a large derelict site within reasonable proximity of the city centre. Work started on the new stadium in 1996 and the ground opened in August 1997. The new ground had a capacity of 42,000, making it the then largest new stadium to be constructed in Britain since the end of World War 2.

Although the new ground — called the Stadium of Light — was initially to see First Division football, Sunderland soon reclaimed their place in the top flight of English football, finishing champions of the First Division at the end of 1998/99. Work started during the following season on the construction of a second tier over the North (Vaux) Stand, adding some 4,500 to the ground's capacity. This work was completed during the 2000/01 season and resulted in the Stadium of Light reaching a current capacity of 48,300. This was to be the first phase of a plan ultimately to see the ground's capacity increased to 64,000 (involving the construction of second tiers on the South and McEwans stands), although completion of this work has no timescale and presumably is dependent upon the Black Cats regaining Premiership status, as the team was relegated at the end of 2002/03.

Left: 1992 (613574)
Below: 2001 (688652)

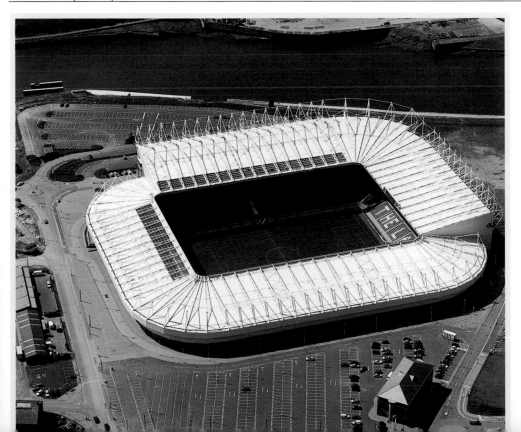

Swansea City

Then: 3 May 1975
Now: 1992

The Vetch Field dates back as a sporting venue to the early 1890s, but it was not until 7 September 1912 that the newly formed Swansea Town — it only became Swansea City in 1970 — played its first game there. The club joined the Football League in 1920 and has, since then, played in all four divisions of the Football League, including two heady years when the Swans played in the old First Division. The 'Then' photograph dates from those heady days of the mid-1970s and shows the ground almost at its peak. The South Stand was constructed in 1913; it was later extended, as shown here, and linked to the West Stand. The West Stand — the Richardson Street End — was constructed in 1927. The North Bank was extended and 1925 and received its cover in 1958. There have been developments at the Vetch over the past 25 years, but the club has been constrained both by opposition to redevelopment and by plans, which are still progressing, for a complete relocation. The North Bank is largely unchanged; an application in 1992 for redevelopment was strongly opposed by locals and has, therefore, not progressed. A new East Stand was opened in January 1982; this curious structure, with terracing in front of it, curves round towards the still extant Main Stand. This arrangement results in the curious angled pylon required for the floodlighting. In 1985 the upper tier of the West Stand was closed; in 1990, rather than demolish the structure, a new roof enclosing the original upper tier was constructed. This has resulted in the curious structure visible today. The Vetch's capacity is currently 11,500, of which only 3,400 are seated.

Towards the end of the 1990s proposals emerged, following the rejection of proposals to redevelop Vetch Field, for the club to relocate to a new 25,000 capacity ground at Morfa, about two miles from the existing ground. However, continuing delays and the fact that the club was put up for sale by its parent company (Ninth Floor) in the spring of 2001 resulted in little progress on the new ground being made, although the local authority gave planning consent to the construction of the new £75 million stadium in January 2001. Further delays resulted in a modified scheme being announced in April 2003 with the new White Rock Stadium, still built on the site of the old Morfa Stadium, scheduled now to provide accommodation of 20,000 and due to open at the start of the 2005/06 season. The £24 million scheme, largely funded by the council, will also provide a home for the town's RUFC team.

Above: 1975 (AC291197)
Right: 1992 (615405)

Swindon Town

Then: 12 July 1972
Now: 1997

The past 15 years have been a rollercoaster for fans of Swindon Town. First, fans were able to celebrate promotion to the top flight of English football, only to have the prize taken away from them when the club was penalised for illegal payments and relegated two divisions (a penalty which was later reduced to leaving the club in the old Second Division). Later the club did achieve Premiership football, but this was to last only one season before two relegations took the team to the Second Division. A Championship in 1995/96 saw the Robins return to the new First Division, but the club has now been relegated back to the Second Division.

Town was originally formed in 1881 and joined the Southern League in 1894. It first played at the County Ground on 4 September 1896 — having been playing at an adjacent site since 1895 — before joining the Football League in 1920. The 'Then' shot shows the ground as it was in 1972, immediately after the completion of the new North Stand in 1971. Also visible are the Town End, which was covered in 1938, and the Shrivenham Road Side, with the so-called Tattoo Stand. This structure, erected in 1958, replaced an earlier cover dating back to 1932; it gained it name from being reused from the Aldershot Tattoo site.

Apart from the North Stand, which was modified with additional seating in the early 1990s, other changes to have affected the County Ground in the past 25 years include the fitting of seats in the Town End (in 1990) and the construction of the new £1.8 million Intel Stand (with its 5,030 seats) that replaced the Tattoo Stand and which opened in 1994. The original structure was part of the County Ground which fell foul of the safety inspectors after 1985. The club had plans to redevelop the Stratton End; however, an application to construct a stand on the site caused opposition amongst local residents. As a short-term measure and in order to fulfil the requirements that the County Ground be turned into an all-seater stadium, seats were added to the Stratton End in two phases, with the work being completed in 1997. Today the County ground has a capacity of 15,700; there are still plans to redevelop the Stratton End but this is strongly opposed by local residents and, given the club's relegation (at the end of the 1999/00 season) to the Second Division, there is little pressure to redevelop this end. Indeed, both Stratton Bank and Town End are used only as overflow currently. During 1999/00, the club suffered financial difficulties, being rescued at the end of the season by a consortium led by Terry Brady.

Now headed by ex-jockey, Willie Carson, Swindon are progressing with plans to relocate to a new 23,000 all-seater stadium for the start of the 2007/08 season at Shaw Pit, although these plans were cast into doubt in July 2004 when local council rejected them.

Left: 1972 (A234783)
Below: 1997

Torquay United

Then: 1992
Now: 14 February 2002

Torquay United was first established in 1898, but the present club is effectively the result of a merger between that team and Torquay Town, which occurred in 1921 at which time the new team became based at Plainmoor. United became members of the Football League in 1927. The first of these two photographs shows Plainmoor at the start of the era when, under the influence of Mike Bateson, the ground was to see considerable redevelopment. The most conspicuous feature of the 1992 ground is the 1,275-seat Ellacombe End, which was completed in 1992. The Main Stand was initially constructed in 1927 but was extended in the 1950s. Part of the Main Stand was damaged by fire shortly after the Bradford fire of 1985 and reconstructed. Opposite the Main Stand is the partially covered Popular Side; this work was undertaken in the 1950s. The final side of the ground, the Babbacombe End, remained uncovered at this time.

Since the early 1990s, a considerable amount of work has been undertaken at Plainmoor. In 1994 the existing Popular Side cover was replaced. At the same time as the Popular Side was replaced, the detached building previously used for the club's offices — which were transferred to the new Popular Side — was demolished and replaced by the 'Gulls Lodge', which provides accommodation for the club's trainee players. Today, Plainmoor has a capacity of just over 6,000. Covered accommodation at the Babbacombe End, initially planned for completion in 1995, has yet to be constructed and proposals for the construction of a new Main Stand, to provide some 2,500 seats, have also yet to progress.

Below: 1992 (614837)
Right: 2002 (692263)

Tottenham Hotspur

Then: 10 September 1966
Now: 7 May 2003

Although founded as Hotspur FC in 1882, the name was changed to Tottenham Hotspur three years later. The club moved to the future White Hart Lane in 1899, playing its first game there on 4 September 1899. Almost a decade later, in 1908, the club was admitted to the Football League. The ground as illustrated in the first of these photographs portrays White Hart Lane as it had existed for some 30 years, the product of the designs of the famous ground designer Archibald Leitch. Leitch's involvement with the ground started in 1909 with the completion of the West Stand — the structure with the Tottenham Hotspur Football Club lettering. In 1921 the Paxton Road (North) End was covered; this was followed two years later by the Park Lane (South) End. Again both these covers were designed by Leitch. Leitch's final involvement with the ground came in 1934 with the completion of the East Stand. Although floodlighting was first installed in 1953 and seating in the rear parts of both end was completed in the early 1960s, the view here would be recognisable to Leitch and to fans from prewar days.

The 2003 photograph shows the dramatic changes to have affected White Hart Lane over the past 30 — and often controversial — years. Although the Leitch ground was to be modified in 1968 and 1972 when the West Stand was extended to link with both ends, the major transformation of the ground started in 1980 with the demolition of the West Stand; the new structure was opened in February 1982. In 1987 plans were unveiled to refurbish the East Stand; work started on this in March 1989 and the new facility was opened the following October. Like all teams in the top two divisions, Spurs were faced by the need to become all-seater. As a result in 1992 seats were installed in the lower tier of the East Side and in the lower section of the Park Lane End. The final section to be converted was the remainder of the East Side, which was undertaken in 1994 just before the deadline. In the meantime, a new roof was constructed at the Paxton Road End; this was completed in 1993 and, two years later,

the South Stand was constructed. Today, White Hart Lane's capacity is 36,257 (all-seated).

During the 2000/01 season, Alan Sugar, the then chairman, sold a controlling stake in the club to ENIC. The new owners announced in March 2001 that they were investigating the possibility of relocation. Unlike north London rivals Arsenal, however, Tottenham's plans have yet to be fully developed. In October 2001 planning permission was granted for the construction of a third tier on the East Stand, taking capacity to 44,000, as a temporary measure whilst relocation was further investigated. This work, however, had no timescale and has not, as yet, been undertaken. It would appear that the club remains committed to relocation, with the new Wembley one possibility, although there are no definite plans.

Right: 1966 (A167143)
Below: 2003 (695623)

Tranmere Rovers

Then: 1992
Now: 1 March 2002

Like Notts County, Tranmere Rovers undertook the radical transformation of its ground over the space of some nine months and thus, whilst this pair of photographs is only some 10 years apart, the view is dramatically different. Founded in 1884, the club adopted the name Tranmere Rovers in 1885. It moved to Prenton Park in 1912, playing its first game on 9 March 1912. Its previous ground was close by, and the first Main Stand was moved the short distance. The club entered the Third Division (North) in 1921. The ground in 1992 comprised the 1968-built Main Stand, the three-pitch Cowshed covering the Prenton Road West Terrace (this was rebuilt in 1972 after having originally been covered in 1931) and the covered Borough Road Side (this was the result of work undertaken in the 1950s replacing an original cover built in 1920). The fourth side was Benington End, which had been banked to form a Kop in 1913. The flood-lights were those installed as replacements in 1988.

In the early 1980s, Rovers were, like a number of other lower division teams, facing extinction. However,

the club was to survive and prosper. Success, however, brought new challenges, in particular the requirement that the ground be turned into an all-seater stadium. Work started on this in the summer of 1994 and the ground was transformed by March the following year. The old Main Stand is the only part of the 1992 ground to remain, but this too has seen work, with seating now also erected in the former paddock. The ground's capacity today is just under 17,000.

Below: 1992 (612663)
Right: 2002 (692607)

Walsall

Then: 20 October 1971
Now: 2002

One of the first of the second-generation football grounds to be completed was Walsall's new ground at Bescot, which opened on 18 August 1990. This pair of photographs shows the contrasting facilities between Walsall's old ground, Fellows Park, and the new ground. Walsall's early footballing history is complex. It first joined the Football League in 1892, leaving in 1895 only to return in 1896 — the year in which it played its first game at Hillary Street (the ground was not renamed as Fellows Park until 1930) on 1 September of that year — before being not re-elected at the end of the 1900/01 season. Between December 1900 and September 1903 the club was forced to play its matches away from Hillary Street; it took slightly longer to reclaim its Football League position, not being readmitted until 1921. The ground as illustrated here was not quite the final stage of Fellows Park — the Main Stand was extended in 1975 — but shows well the confined site that the club occupied. Both the Main Stand and the covered Popular Side dated from prior to World War 2. The Hillary Street End was covered in 1965; the same year also saw the demolition of the laundry at the Railway (East) End. The laundry had prevented the ground providing accommodation on all four sides and, with its demolition, the opportunity was taken to construct a terrace on this side. The story of the relocation starts in the mid-1980s with a succession of controversial chairmen — Ken Wheldon, Terry Ramsden and Maurice Miller — under whose control the fortunes of the club fluctuated. The story of the relocation is complex; suffice to note here that planning permission for the redevelopment of Fellows Park was granted in August 1986. It was, however, not until 11 May 1990 that the club played its last game at the ground. Following this, the old ground was demolished. The new Bescot Stadium has, today, a capacity of just over 11,500. The Main Stand is named after H. L. Fellows, the stand opposite is known as the Banks' Family Stand (it was previously known as the Highgate Mild Stand). To the left of the Main Stand is the Gilbert Alsop End, which provides terracing for the home supports. The opposite end — named after William Sharp — was originally provided with terracing, but seats were installed in 1992. The next phase in the development of the Bescot Stadium was the reconstruction of the Gilbert Alsop Stand, with the intention of replacing the existing terrace, which could accommodate 2,700, with a two-tier cantilevered stand capable of seating 4,000. The new £2 million Purple Stand was opened on 23 November 2002 and took the ground's capacity to 11,500; this structure was converted to all-seater in 2003. The club has plans to rebuild the William Sharp Stand in a similar style to take the capacity to 13,500 although this work also requires the local authority to grant permission to allow the external wall for advertising. If all is approved, it hoped that the stand will be completed by August 2005.

Far left: 1971 (A220545)
Left: 2002 (692722)

Watford

Then: 30 June 1972
Now: 16 June 2003

Few football clubs can claim to have had a chairman as colourful as Elton John, but there is no doubt that he and Graham Taylor have in their various stints with the club radically altered the face of Vicarage Road, both as a stadium and in terms of success on the field. Although the club has its origins in the 1880s, it was not until 1920 that Watford joined the Third Division of the Football League and not until 30 August 1922 did it play its first game at Vicarage Road. The 'Then' shot, albeit dating from the early 1970s, shows the ground very much as it developed in 1920. At the centre of the East Side was a 45yd-long stand (this was extended to the south in 1969). Opposite was the Shrodells (West) Stand; this had been transferred from the earlier Cassio Road ground as had the short cover at the Rookery (South) End. The Vicarage Road End was built up with hard-core (later concreted) for terracing and concrete terracing was also installed between the Shrodells Stand and the Rookery End (in the 1930s). The ground's shape also owes much to the fact that, from 1928 until 1969 and from 1975 until it finally ceased in 1978, Vicarage Road was used for greyhound racing. There have been radical changes to Vicarage Road over the past quarter of a century. Although the Main Stand and its 1969 extension survive, these have been fitted with seats throughout. The first phase of the ground's modernisation came with the opening of the Sir Stanley Rous (West) Stand on 18 October 1986. This

was followed in October 1993 by the opening of the North Stand (replacing the Vicarage Road Terrace) and in March 1995 by the new South Stand (replacing the Rookery End). At the end of the 2003/04 season Watford had a capacity of 20,150 all seated. This was significantly reduced in the summer of 2004 by the enforced closure of the old East Stand. Whilst the club had planned previously to rebuild the East Stand (with a new 4,500-seat structure), the club's financial position, exacerbated by the demise of ITV Digital, meant that the project was put on ice. With the club struggling in the League Championship and with crowds currently averaging below the new maximum, the club may decide to hold fire on any reconstruction; however, if finances improve or if promotion to the Premiership becomes a possibility then the club will need to take action to replace the stand.

Below: 2003 (695966)
Right: 1972 (A235427)

West Bromwich Albion

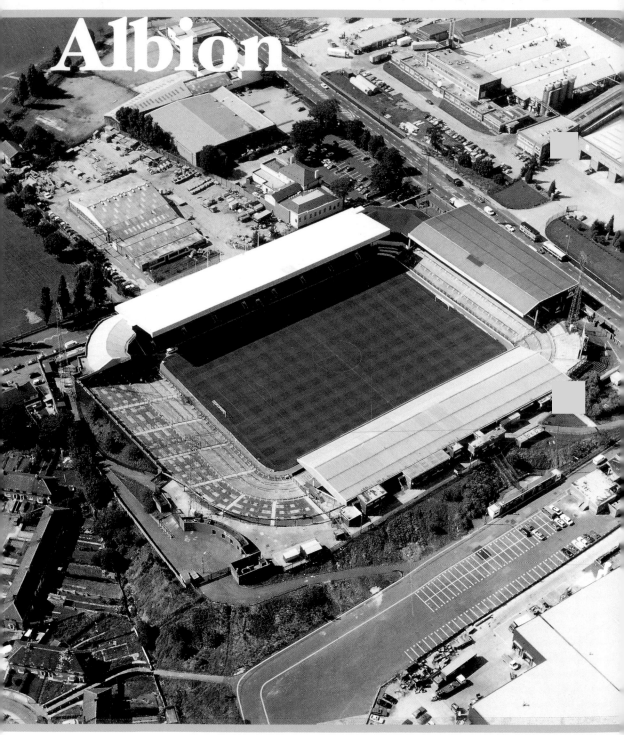

Then: 1992
Now: 12 March 2002

Although these two photographs are but a decade apart, they do show well the rapidity of change at British football stadia during the 1980s and 1990s as teams in the top two divisions have faced the imperative of becoming all-seater. West Bromwich Albion, one of the founder members of the Football League in 1888, were established as the West Bromwich Strollers in 1879, becoming Albion two years later. After a number of grounds played host to the team, the club moved to a new site — which became known as 'The Hawthorns' — in 1900, playing its first game there on 3 September 1900. The 'Then' photograph shows, nearest to the camera, the Smethwick Road End; although this had been reroofed as late as 1985 — following the Bradford fire — the roof was dismantled in 1992. Opposite, is the Birmingham Road End; this had been covered in 1964 when part of the cover from the old Handsworth Side was transferred when the so-called Rainbow Stand was being constructed. The corner stand linking the Main Stand with the Smethwick Road End was constructed in 1934; the Main Stand itself — the Halford's Road Stand — was the result of rebuilding work between 1979 and 1981, which replaced the 1939 rebuild of the original structure. The corner stand linking the Main Stand with the Birmingham

Road End was constructed in 1958. Apart from the Main Stand, which still survives, the major changes have affected both ends and the Rainbow Stand. The Smethwick Road End was cleared in January 1994 with the new stand opening in September that year. The Birmingham Road End was demolished in April 1994, with the new stand opening in the following December. Work on the next phase of the reconstruction of The Hawthorns commenced during the 2000/01 season with the demolition in January 2001 of the 1964-built Rainbow Stand to make way for a new 8,000-seat stand costing £5 million. Once completed, this took the capacity of The Hawthorns to about 28,000. The design of the new stand permits the construction of a second tier should this be required. The club has long-term plans to increase the ground's capacity to 40,000. In order to further these, it has acquired the Woodman Pub, located between the Apollo and East stands, and plans to demolish it, replacing it with a 2,000-seat corner stand. There are also plans to redevelop the Halford's Lane Stand.

Left: 1992 (612641)
Below: 2002 (692729)

West Bromwich Albion

177

West Ham United

Then: 10 June 1965
Now: 18 February 2002

As with a number of other 'Then' shots, this photograph of the Boleyn Ground — as Upton Park should be properly called — shows work in progress in 1965 extending the West Stand by an additional bay to the south. This photograph also shows well how confined the area occupied by the ground was and how important, for the future of the club, that it was able to expand the site by acquiring land to the north. West Ham United was formed as Thames Ironworks in September 1895 and joined the Southern League in 1898. The club became West Ham United in 1900 and moved to the Boleyn Ground in May 1904, playing its first game there on 1 September the same year. The Hammers joined the Football League in 1919. The ground in 1965 comprised the double-deck West Stand, which was originally built in 1925 and which is being extended here. The South Bank roof was transferred from the old (1913) West Stand in 1925; this suffered war damage in 1944 but was repaired. The North Bank was covered in 1961. Finally, the narrow East Side was covered during the mid-1920s; as a result of the materials used in the building's construction, it became known as the 'Chicken Run'. The more recent photograph shows developments over a near 40-year period. First, in May 1968 the 'Chicken Run' was demolished to be replaced by a new East Stand which opened in January 1968; this structure was fully fitted with seats in 1994. In the mid-1970s seats were fitted in the West Stand paddock and the capacity in the North Bank was reduced as the ground became governed by the Safety at Sports Grounds Act. The major development, however, came after the acquisition of the old school site in 1991 and the launch of the highly controversial bond scheme. The £5.5 million Bobby Moore (North) Stand — named after the late West Ham and England captain — was opened in February 1994. The South Bank was demolished in May 1993 with the new Centenary Stand being opened in February 1995. The work in the mid-1990s resulted in the ground having a capacity of just over 26,000, making it relatively small in Premiership terms and the club developed plans for the further expansion of the stadium. Work started on the new West Stand in January 2001. This new stand — called the Dr Martens Stand — was completed by the start of the 2001/02 season and saw the ground's capacity increased from 26,100 to 35,000. Following this work, the club plans to rebuild the East Stand and undertake work on the Bobby Moore and Centenary stands, raising the capacity to more than 40,000. The total cost of these new stands is £35 million and work has been deferred on the next phase now that the team has been relegated to the League Championship.

Below: 2002 (692163)
Right: 1965 (A150665)

178

Wigan Athletic

Then: 4 October 1972
Now: 2000

Although Springfield Park opened in 1897 and was first used for a football match on 1 September of that year, professional football in Wigan had a somewhat chequered career until May 1932 when Wigan Athletic was formed. Prior to Athletic, Wigan Borough, which had been formed in November 1920, had joined the Third Division (North) of the Football League in 1921; this club, however, collapsed in October 1931. It was, however, during Borough's occupation of Springfield Park that much development work was undertaken. During the 1920s, a 2,000-seat Main Stand was built — this was destroyed by fire in May 1953 and replaced in mid-1954 by the stand illustrated in the 'Then' photograph — as were covers over the rear of the Shevington End and along the Popular Side. Floodlighting was installed in 1966. After many years of campaigning, Athletic were finally elected to the Football League in 1978. Over the next quarter century there were only

relatively minor improvements at the ground. The small covered area at the Shevington End disappeared and in 1994 the Popular Side was reroofed and terraced, with barriers acquired second-hand from Villa Park. The curved ends behind both goal posts are a reflection of the time when Springfield Park was also used for cycle racing and athletics. By the late 1990s, the capacity at Springfield Park was some 7,466 but the club had already developed plans to relocate and construct a new ground, in conjunction with the town's Rugby League team, at Robin Park. The new ground — the JJB Stadium — opened in August 1999 and provides a 25,000 all-seated capacity. The impressive new ground which is shared by the town's Rugby League team, is illustrated in the 'Now' photograph.

Left: 2000 (685062)
Below: 1972 (A247054)

Wolverhampton Wanderers

Then: 29 April 1972
Now: 9 February 2004

Without doubt one of the great names of English football, Wolverhampton Wanderers — one of the founder members of the Football League — were already a decade old when the club moved into the existing Molineux ground in 1889. The first game was played there on 2 September of that year. The first of these two photographs shows the original alignment of the ground prior to the traumas of the 1980s when the club plummeted down to the old Fourth Division and almost went out of business. The ground as illustrated here was largely the result of developments after 1921 when the great designer Archibald Leitch was employed. The Main Stand along Waterloo Road, with its paddock, was opened on 12 September 1925. The North Bank was remodelled in the early 1930s, whilst the new Molineux Street Stand, with its seven-pitch roof, was opened in 1932. This was followed in 1935 by the construction of a roof over part of the South Bank and by the construction of an extension — not visible in the photograph — behind the Waterloo Stand.

The redevelopment of Molineux, evident in the more recent photograph, began after the Molineux Street Stand was condemned as a result of the 1975 Safety of Sports Grounds Act. The club acquired the property behind the stand and demolished the existing structure, replacing it with the John Ireland Stand which was set back from the existing pitch to allow for a future realignment and which opened on 25 May 1979. In the event it was to be more than a decade before this plan could be realised. In 1985, after the Bradford Fire, the North Bank terrace and the Waterloo Street Stand were both condemned, but worse was to follow in 1986 when the club went into receivership. That it survived at all reflects well on the local council and on a deal struck with a developer. The ground today, however, is the result of the involvement of Sir Jack Hayward, who, in April 1991, guaranteed the costs of rebuilding the ground. In October 1991 the North Bank was

demolished, to be replaced with the £2 million Stan Cullis (now Steve Bull) Stand; it was at this time that the pitch was realigned. In May 1992 the Waterloo Road Stand was demolished, being replaced with the Billy Wright Stand opened in August 1993. Finally, the old South Bank was cleared in mid-1993, with the John Harris Stand opening on 7 December the same year. That same year also saw a partial refurbishment of the John Ireland Stand. For the team's promotion to the Premiership, for the 2003/04 season, temporary seating for 900 was added between the Jack Harris and Billy Wright stands. Today, Molineux has a capacity of 29,400 and is a truly impressive stadium; a far cry from the dark days of the early 1980s. The club has plans to add second tiers to both ends of the ground and rebuild the Steve Bull Stand, taking the total capacity to 40,000. However, this work will require the club to regaining — and retaining this time — its place in the Premiership.

Below: 2004 (696909)

Right: 1972 (A235331)

Wrexham

Then: 1976
Now: 2000

The Racecourse Ground at Wrexham is one of the oldest venues to be featured in this book, dating back originally to 1807 when it was used for horse racing. This activity continued until 1858 and then again between 1873 and 1912. Football was first played at the ground in 1872, although the current club was not established until April 1884 as Wrexham Olympic, becoming simply Wrexham in 1887. The club joined the Football League in 1921. The first of these two photographs shows the Racecourse Ground as it existed in the mid-1970s. In 1971 it was decided that the existing ground would be modernised and the first result of this scheme was the Yale Stand, furthest from to the camera, which replaced the original covered Popular Side in 1972. To the left of the Yale Stand was the Town End; the small stand — known as the Pigeon Loft — was installed in 1962. This structure had been acquired from a local cinema and was destined to survive until 1978. Opposite the Yale Stand was the original Main (Mold Road) Stand, which dated back to 1902. This structure had been extended with the wing stand — the Plas Coch Stand — at an angle during the 1930s. The first section of the Plas Coch (West) End had been covered in 1926 and the complete end followed three years later. Floodlighting was installed in 1959.

The Racecourse Ground was, as a result of the safety scares of the 1980s, a three-sided affair for a number of years with the Mold Road side closed since 1985. The old Mold Road side was demolished during 1999 and replaced by the new 3,500-seat Pryce Griffiths Stand. The original Plas Coch End was replaced with a new 2,250-seat stand in December 1978. The Town End Terrace received a new cover in 1980 following the demolition of the Pigeon Loft. For a short period — between October 1992 and March 1993 — the Town End was fenced off as a preliminary to a redevelopment; in the event this did not materialise. The ground's capacity is currently almost 16,000 of which just over 11,000 are seated. Following the construction of the Pryce Griffiths Stand, the next phase of redevelopment work at the Racecourse Ground was to have featured the Kop End Terrace. However, during the summer of 2004, the club's new owners announced that it was looking at a major redevelopment of the Racecourse Ground, involving rotating the pitch 90°; there is, however, no timescale at present.

Left: 1976 (320971)
Below: 2000 (685073)

Wycombe Wanderers

Then: 21 January 1972
Now: 27 March 2002

Founded towards the end of the 19th century, the team became known as Wycombe Wanderers in 1887. The team moved to a ground called Loakes Park courtesy of the then Lord Carrington, playing the first game there on 7 September 1895. This is the ground that is illustrated in the first of the two photographs. The first stand to be built at the ground was constructed in 1903-4. In 1921 Wycombe joined the Isthmian League and this was followed, in January 1923, by the opening of a new main stand as illustrated here. A decade later, in February 1932, the terrace opposite the main stand was covered. In 1947, through the generous support of Frank Adams, the club was able to acquire the freehold of the Loakes Park ground; in retrospect this was a crucial factor in the development of the club as, when it was decided to move to a new ground, the sale of the old ground helped raise the funds required to build the new ground. After a period of searching for a new location, Wanderers found the site of the future Adams Park — named after the benefactor of the 1940s — in the mid-1980s, but it was not until 1990 that the new ground was completed. The last game at Loakes Park, against an international 11, was played on 7 May 1990 and the first game at the new ground was played on 9 August 1990. The site of the original ground was sold to developers, with part being used for housing and part being used for an extension to the local hospitals. As originally constructed, Adams Park had a capacity of 8,000 with covered accommodation on all four sides, although this was later increased to 10,000 with the addition of extra barriers on the terracing. At the end of the 1992/93 season Wanderers achieved promotion to the Football League; the team is

currently in League Two, having achieved promotion through the Play Offs at the end of the club's first season in the League but being relegated at the end of 2003/04. Since the completion of Adams Park the ground has undergone major change in the replacement of the Woodlands Terrace with a new stand. This new structure, which took the ground's capacity to 10,000, was opened in 1997. The next phase in the expansion of Adams Park — renamed the Causeway Stadium during 2003/04 — was the erection of a second tier over the Roger Vere Stand. This kept the ground's capacity to 10,000, but increased the seating total to 8,250.

Below: 1972 (A221478)
Right: 2002 (692826)

Yeovil Town

Then: 1935
Now: 6 May 2003

One of the most famous names in non-league football, Yeovil Town finally achieved promotion to the Football League at the end of the 2002/03 season. The origins of the club date back to the late 19th century, when a team called Yeovil Casuals played at a ground near Pen Mill station. The team was retitled 'Town' in 1908 and adopted the now well-known colours of green and white. A merger with another local team occurred in 1914, with the new team continuing to play at Town's original ground. The club moved to The Huish Athletic Ground in 1920 and relocated the stand from Pen Mill to provide the first covered accommodation. The stand was extended in 1922; the end terraces were built up simultaneously. In 1924 the Brutton Road end was terraced and, in November 1926, the Queen Street End was covered. Initial moves to relocate from The Huish commenced in March 1985, although work was not to begin on construction of the new ground until after the publication of the public enquiry — held in 1987 — in February 1989. The new ground was provided with two full length stands, seating a toal of 5,200, with uncovered terraces at either end providing standing accommodation for a further 4,200, giving the ground a total capacity of 9,400.

Below: 1935 (48468)
Right: 2003 (695574)

Then: 24 August 1959
Now: 30 April 2001

There are few stadia more famous than Wembley and more redolent of sporting triumph; for many sportsman, particularly in football and Rugby League, playing at Wembley was the pinnacle of their playing ambitions and for fans, seeing their team walk out on the Wembley pitch epitomised everything that a supporter desires. Any fan, who has seen their team triumph at Wembley, will retain the memories for many years. It was the venue for the FA Cup Final since 1923 and the number of other domestic games played at Wembley increased over the years, including the Play Off finals; apart from these games, Wembley was the home base of the England football team and was also used for 1948 Olympic Games, the 1966 World Cup and, more recently, the European Football Championships in 1996.

Despite its pedigree, however, Wembley was increasingly showing its age; modern regulations had seen the ground's capacity cut and work was due to start in 2001 on the wholesale redevelopment of the ground. In order to gain National Lottery funding for the construction of a new national stadium, ownership of Wembley was transferred to the English National Stadium Trust during 1998. Once the transfer was completed, plans for the ground's redevelopment were, in theory, finalised but problems over the cost

of the scheme resulted in delays. Work on the new stadium now proceeds apace with a planned opening in 2006 (see photograph on page 3).

The first of these two photographs shows Wembley as it existed from construction in the early 1920s through to its complete reroofing 40 years later. The vast open terraces are a reminder of the era when the ground's capacity was 100,000, although the record attendance was 126,047 for the first FA Cup Final to be staged at the ground (between West Ham and Bolton Wanderers) in 1923. The ground was fully covered in 1963; at that time some 44,000 of the ground's capacity was seated. Wembley became an all-seater stadium in 1990 and, in order to provide an additional 4,000 seats, the Olympic Gallery was constructed. Since the late 1980s some £40 million had been spent at Wembley, resulting in an all-seater capacity of 80,000.

With the demise of Wembley — at least temporarily — the FA selected the Millennium Stadium in Cardiff as the location for cup and Play Off finals and the second of these two photographs shows the impressive stadium. Built on the site of the world-famous Cardiff Arms Park, traditional home of Welsh rugby, the Millennium Stadium, with its 75,000 capacity, opened for the 2000 Rugby Union World Cup. Boasting a retractable roof, the stadium has played host to the FA Cup final and other major fixtures.

Far left: 1959 (A78097)
Left: 2001 (688016)

Aerofilms

Aerofilms was founded in 1919 and has specialised in the acquisition of aerial photography within the United Kingdom throughout its history. The company has a record of being innovative in the uses and applications of aerial photography.

Photographs looking at the environment in perspective are called oblique aerial photographs. These are taken with Hasselblad cameras by professional photographers experienced in the difficult conditions encountered in aerial work.

Photographs taken straight down at the landscape are termed vertical aerial photographs. These photographs are obtained using Leica survey cameras, the products from which are normally used in the making of maps.

Aerofilms has a unique library of oblique and vertical photographs in excess of one and a half million in number covering the United Kingdom. This library of photographs dates from 1919 to the present day and is being continually updated.

Oblique and vertical photography can be taken to customers' specification by Aerofilms' professional photographers.

To discover more of the wealth of past or present photographs held in the library at Aerofilms or to commission new aerial photographs, please contact:

Simmons Aerofilms
32-34 Station Close
Potters Bar
Herts EN6 1TL

Telephone: 01707 648390
Fax: 01707 648399
Web-site: www.simmonsaerofilms.com
E-mail: info@aerofilms.com

Wembley/
Millennium
Stadium